Presented to

_____

By

_____

On the Occasion of

_____

_____ , 19____

By Helen Steiner Rice

Helen Steiner Rice

Gifts From the Heart

Fleming H. Revell Company
Old Tappan, New Jersey

The pastel portrait by Eileen Annest
on the back flap of this book was pre-
sented to Mrs. Rice on her eightieth
birthday and is suitable for framing.

Book Design and Illustrations by
John Okladek

Library of Congress Cataloging in Publication Data

Rice, Helen Steiner.
  Gifts from the heart.

  1. Religious poetry, American.   I. Title.
PS3568.I28G54   811'.54   81-249
ISBN 0-8007-1261-7   AACR2
ISBN 0-8007-1262-5 (keepsake)

ISBN 0-8007-1261-7
ISBN 0-8007-1262-5 (Keepsake ed.)
Copyright © 1981 Fleming H. Revell Company
All rights reserved
Printed in the United States of America

My Thanks!

People everywhere in life
    from every walk and station,
From every town and city
    and every state and nation
Have given me so many things
    intangible and dear,
I couldn't begin to count them all
    or even make them clear . . .
I only know I owe so much
    to people everywhere
And when I put my thoughts in verse
    it's just a way to share
The musings of a thankful heart,
    a heart much like your own,
For nothing that I think or write
    is mine and mine alone . . .
So if you found some beauty
    in any word or line,
It's just "Your Soul's Reflection"
    in "Proximity with Mine."

HELEN STEINER RICE

Contents

Foreword

The New York Times has acclaimed Helen Steiner Rice as "The Inspirational Poet Laureate of America." Millions around the world have purchased her greeting cards and books. One hundred million viewers have heard her poems read on the Lawrence Welk Show. For half a century she has been on the writing staff of Gibson Greeting Cards in Cincinnati. Countless persons have made her verses a part of their joy-filled moments and have been uplifted by her words of encouragement during times of heartache and tragedy.

What is Helen Steiner Rice's response to the tremendous impact her poems have had on readers everywhere? In a recent interview she said, "These are not *my* poems. These are God's answers to people's needs. I am just His instrument, His messenger."

Over years of close publisher-author contact with this lovely little lady, we have been impressed by Mrs. Rice's unique ability to select the most suitable topics and verses for each of her books. Further, she has a keen sense of the appropriate in her judgment of book and jacket design and title. Along the way from concept to completed volume, prayer is a part of each decision, of each problem. Later, as the book moves from one printing to the next, Mrs. Rice praises God and gives Him the glory.

God's presence is clearly evident at every meeting with Mrs. Rice. Fairness, unselfishness, giving, helping, consoling, reaching out, serving — these are the key words in her vocabulary.

While leaders in industry, politics, education, and in the worlds of entertainment and literature have sought out her friendship, Mrs. Rice has more often given of herself to the "near greats"—the countergirl at the coffee shop, the machine operator at the plant, the clerk at the office, the chambermaid at the hotel, the bookstore salesperson. In the language of today's youth, Mrs. Rice "walks the talk." Truly, each day she *lives* the love about which she writes so often.

The Fleming H. Revell Company staff joins with her friends everywhere in extending our special greetings to Helen Steiner Rice on her eightieth birthday.

Corrie ten Boom, author of *The Hiding Place*, and also in her eighties, once said, "Accepting Christ is not an end, but a beginning. There is a second step. We must accept Him as our Lord. When we do this, He lives His victorious life in us—He the vine, we the branches. The branch without the vine has no value at all. The vine has everlasting value. When connected with the vine, the branch bears fruit." By serving as just such a "branch," Helen Steiner Rice's lifelong ministry-in-verse has indeed borne a world-sized basket of magnificent fruit!

The Publishers

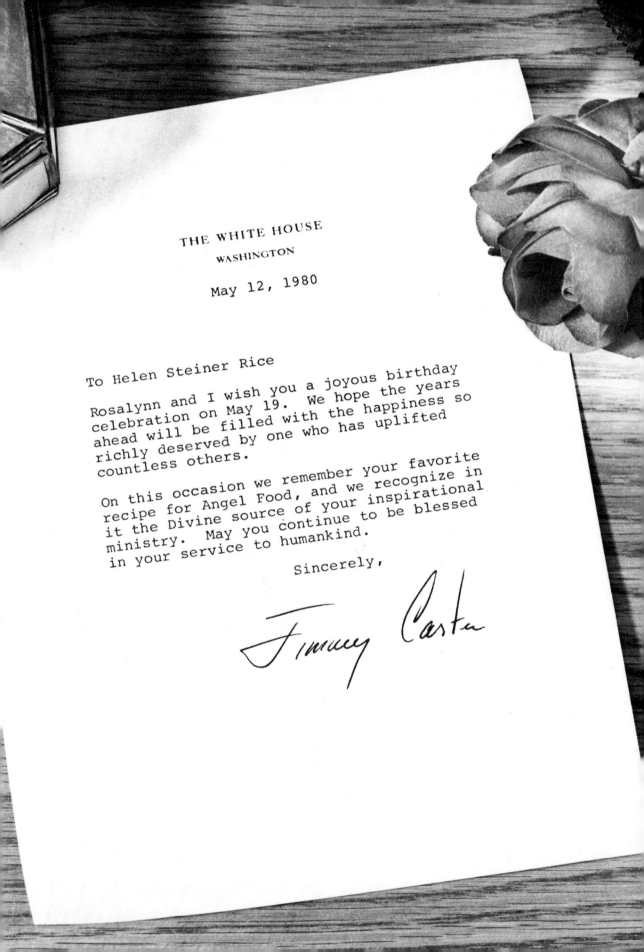

THE WHITE HOUSE

WASHINGTON

May 12, 1980

To Helen Steiner Rice

Rosalynn and I wish you a joyous birthday celebration on May 19. We hope the years ahead will be filled with the happiness so richly deserved by one who has uplifted countless others.

On this occasion we remember your favorite recipe for Angel Food, and we recognize in it the Divine source of your inspirational ministry. May you continue to be blessed in your service to humankind.

Sincerely,

Jimmy Carter

May 14, 1980

Ron Kidwell, Shop Steward, Lo
ternational Union of Electrical W
Earl Keihl, Director, District
Furniture Workers.
Ted Krukowski, Vice Presi
United Electrical Work
Ellen C. Lavrof
eration of T
Jam

JOHN GLENN
OHIO

FOREIGN RE
GOVERNMEN
SPECIAL COMMITTEE

United States Senate

WASHINGTON. D.C. 20510

May 19, 1980

Mrs. Helen Steiner Rice
Gibson Greeting Cards Inc.
2100 Section Road
Cincinnati, OH 45202

Dear Mrs. Rice:

I am pleased to join your many friends, colleagues
and family members in wishing you a very happy birthday
and in congratulating you on Helen Steiner Rice Day
in Cincinnati. These are important milestones!

Your distinguished career at Gibson Greeting Cards
as well as the help and inspiration you have provided for
thousands of people throughout the United States are
well known, not only to Cincinnatians, but to men
and women everywhere. We're proud to have such a
distinguished citizen of Ohio, and I am honored to
join everyone in saying: many happy returns of the day.

May the years ahead continue to be fulfilling and
purposeful.

Best regards, Mrs. Rice.

Sincerely,

John Glenn
United States Senator

In-
ed

4. All members shall have the right to
vote on dues, establish union salaries and
control the expenditure of union monies.

5. All unions shall take special steps to
guarantee representation by Black, Latin
and women members on all policy-making
bodies.

6. All union members shall have the right
to respect the picket lines of other workers.

7. All workers shall have the right to join
and participate in union affairs without
regard to race, creed, national origin or po-
litical belief or affiliation.

8. Members shall have the right to all
union documents in his/her own language.●

DEPARTMENT OF DEFENSE AUTHORIZATION ACT, 1981—I

SPEECH OF

HON. BILL NICHOLS
OF ALABAMA

IN THE HOUSE OF REPRESENTATIVES

Tuesday, May 13, 1980

The House in Committee of the Whole
House on the State of the Union had under
consideration the bill (H.R 6974) to author-
ize appropriations for fiscal year 1981 for
procurement of aircraft, missiles, naval ves-
sels and combat vehicles, torpedoes, and
other weapons and for research, develop-
ment, and evaluation for the Armed
Forces; to prescribe the authorized person-
nel strength for each active duty component
and the Selected Reserve of each Reserve
component of the Armed Forces and for ci-
vilian personnel of the Department of De-
fense; to authorize the military training stu-
dent loads; authorize appropriations for
civil defense, and for

RDS of Alabama. Mr.
..., I commend the gen-
...work in this field, and I
...entleman from Wash-
...s) for his persistence
...ue and his pursuit of
...ajor problem in our

N. The time of the
... Alabama   (Mr.
...d.

N. Mr. Chairman, I
...e gentleman from
...s).

... Alabama. If the
...urther, I wonder
... also going to
...this regard into
...cy pay.

...oblems we have
...hanics, for ex-
... school, they
...ics, they can
...-15, the heli-
...ir specialty,
...ment time
...te industry
...cent more,
...ns, and all

at that

...nan, let
... saying
...urrence
...major
...articu-

---

larly with our non-commissioned offi-
cers, whom I look at as the Phi Beta
Kappas in commons... in today's
military.

I would say to the gentleman, that
the gentleman from Texas (Mr.
WHITE), chairman of the Subcommit-
tee on Military Personnel, and our
own committee, are very much inter-
ested in that aspect of the particular
matter that the gentleman brings to
our attention. It would be my inten-
tion to devote a good bit of time to
that in the weeks ahead.

Mr. EDWARDS of Alabama. I thank
the gentleman.

TRIBUTE TO HELEN STEINER RICE

HON. THOMAS A. LUKEN
OF OHIO

IN THE HOUSE OF REPRESENTATIVES

Wednesday, May 14, 1980

● Mr. LUKEN. Mr. Speaker, Emerson
said, "We do not count a man's years
until he has nothing else to count."
This quote is certainly true of Helen
Steiner Rice, who has so much to
count that her years seem few.

It was Cincinnati's good fortune
when she came here to work at the
Gibson Greeting Card Co. in 1931. We
feel privileged to have had her career
bloom and grow in our city. But Mrs.
Rice's special touch with words has
reached well beyond our city. Her
words have been published in Europe,
Africa, the Philippines, New Zealand,
and Canada, as well as in the United
States. Her words have brought cheer,
comfort, hope, and inspiration to mil-
lions of people around the world. They
have brought, also, our respect and
pride.

Her birthday on May 19, 1980, gives
me the opportunity to note her many
contributions and to thank her for the
rich use of her talents. We are en-
riched and inspired by her work.●

ALABAMA LEGISLATURE CALLS FOR PROLIFE AMENDMENT

HON. JOHN M. ASHBROOK
OF OHIO

IN THE HOUSE OF REPRESENTATIVES

Wednesday, May 14, 1980

● Mr. ASHBROOK. Mr. Speaker, on
April 23, by a House vote of 65 to 16,
Alabama became the 19th State to call
upon Congress to convene a constitu-
tional convention to propose a human
life amendment to the U.S. Constitu-
tion.

I would like to point out the obvious
fact that Alabama is not one of our
more overwhelmingly Catholic States.
Once again, the bigotted stereotyping
of prolife as a Catholic phenomenon is
exposed for the nonsense it is. A
simple look at the States which have
called for a human life amendment
would destroy this stereotype in the

... his
...con-
...hah
...ews
...ary
...tin-
...olu-
...ied:
...the
...nit
...illi-
...his
...yal

...ser
...he
...to
...he
...t a
...a's
...um

...nt
...re
...es
...w

...to
...ry
...e-
...n.
...ip
...il
...i.
...i.
...n

...r
...e
..."

...a

...e-
...er,
...0
...n

...r
...e

HELEN STEINER RICE

HON. WILLIS D. GRADISON, JR.
OF OHIO

IN THE HOUSE OF REPRESENTATIVES

Tuesday, April 29, 1980

● Mr. GRADISON. Mr. Speaker, on
May 19, Mrs. Helen Steiner Rice, the
"poet laureate of the greeting card
world," will celebrate her 80th birth-
day in Cincinnati. As her coworkers at
Gibson Greeting Cards and her
friends and admirers from around the
country gather to mark this occasion,
I wanted to salute Mrs. Rice and make
my colleagues aware of some of her
achievements.

Before joining Gibson Greeting
Cards in 1931, Mrs. Rice had already
established a reputation as a speaker
of great force for women's rights and
their place in the business world. As
Gibson's editorial director, she strove
for more meaningful expression in
greeting cards. In 1960, after one of
her poems was read on the Lawrence
Welk Show, the demand for her
poetry exploded.

To date, Mr. Speaker, her work has
appeared in over 75 million greeting
cards, 14 hard-cover books, and 17
booklets. These materials have been
published in Europe, Africa, Australia,
the Philippines, New Zealand, and
Canada, in addition to their wide cir-
culation in the United States.

As you can well imagine, Mr. Speak-
er, the nature of Mrs. Rice's verse and
its wide circulation have won her a de-
voted following around the world. Mrs.
Rice carries on an extensive corre-
spondence with individuals from all
walks of life who seek her guidance,
inspiration, and solace. Until a recent
accident, she regularly came to her
office at Gibson to write verse, answer
her correspondence, and edit her
books. She has recently published her
autobiography, "In the Vineyard of
the Lord."

Mr. Speaker, I join the 2,000 employ-
ees of Gibson Greeting Cards, all Cin-
cinnatians, and Mrs. Rice's admirers
and friends around the world in wish-
ing her a joyous 80th birthday and
continued success in her "greeting
card ministry."●

FLAGS OVER THE C...

HON. ...

HOUSE OF REPRESENTATIVES
WASHINGTON, D.C. 20515

THOMAS A. LUKEN
2ND DISTRICT OHIO

May 13, 1980

Helen Steiner Rice
Gibson Greeting Card Company
2100 Section Road
Cincinnati, Ohio 45237

Dear Mrs. Rice:

Emerson said, " We do not count a man's years until he has nothing else to count." This quote is certainly true for your birthday. You have so much to count that your years seem few.

It was Cincinnati's good fortune when you came here to work for the Gibson Greeting Card Company in 1931. We feel privileged to have had your career bloom and grow in our city. But your special touch with words has reached well beyond Cincinnati. Your published works have brought cheer, comfort, hope and inspiration to millions of people around the world. And your works- also bring our respect and pride.

Your birthday gives me the opportunity to note your many contributions and to thank you for the rich use of your talents. We are enriched and inspired by your work.

Sincerely,

Thomas A. Luken
Member of Congress

STATE OF OHIO
OFFICE OF THE GOVERNOR
COLUMBUS 43215

JAMES A. RHODES
GOVERNOR

May 15, 1980

Mrs. Helen Steiner Rice
Gibson Greeting Cards, Inc.
2100 Section Road
Cincinnati, Ohio 45237

Dear Mrs. Rice:

Noting special occasions is a pleasant task for me as Ohio's governor. I would therefore like to take this opportunity to congratulate you and extend to you my personal best wishes as you celebrate your 80th birthday on May 19.

As the poet laureate of the greeting card industry, you are an inspiration to the many people around the world who maintain a high regard for you and your work. Your many years at Gibson are a tribute to those such as you, who use their God-given talents for the joy and enlightenment of others. The people of Ohio can be proud of your continuing accomplishments.

Sincerely,

JAMES A. RHODES
Governor

/jad

PASSED: 1/14/80

BY: STEINBERG

RESOLUTION NO. C-405

RESOLUTION COMMENDING HELEN STEINER RICE
FOR HER CONTRIBUTIONS AND DEDICATION
TO HUMANITY IN THIS HER 80TH YEAR

WHEREAS, Helen Steiner Rice, being born on the 19th day
of May, 1900, has resided in Cincinnati since 1931, making notable
contributions as a writer, and

WHEREAS, her writings, which have cheered and comforted
people in all walks of life all over the world, as well as her
many humanitarian efforts and charitable contributions, deserve
recognition.

NOW, THEREFORE, BE IT RESOLVED BY THE COUNCIL OF THE
VILLAGE OF AMBERLEY VILLAGE, STATE OF OHIO, Six (6) Members
elected thereto concurring:

SECTION 1: That the Village Council hereby recognizes
and publicly acknowledges in this her 80th year the many contribu-
tions and humanitarian dedication of Helen Steiner Rice to her
fellow persons.

SECTION 2: That the Council hereby formally record its
acknowledgement, appreciation and gratitude to Helen Steiner Rice
on behalf of the many persons so moved by her selfless contributions
and devotion to mankind.

SECTION 3: That the Clerk of Council be, and she hereby
is authorized and directed to prepare a counterpart of this Resolu-
tion to evidence its adoption, said counterpart to be signed by the
Mayor and attested by the Clerk, and to be presented to Helen
Steiner Rice.

SECTION 4: That this Resolution shall take effect and be
in force from and after the earliest period allowable by law.

Passed this 14th day of January, 1980.

ATTEST:

Betty Sizemore
Clerk of Council

Arthur H. Friedman, Mayor
Arthur H. Friedman, Mayor

I, Clerk of Council of the Village of Amberley Village,
Ohio, certify that on the 7th day of February, 1980, the
foregoing Resolution was published pursuant to Article IX of the
Home Rule Charter by posting true copies of said Resolution at all
of the places of public notice as designated by Sec. 30.04(A),
Code of Ordinances.

Betty Sizemore
Betty Sizemore,
Clerk of Council

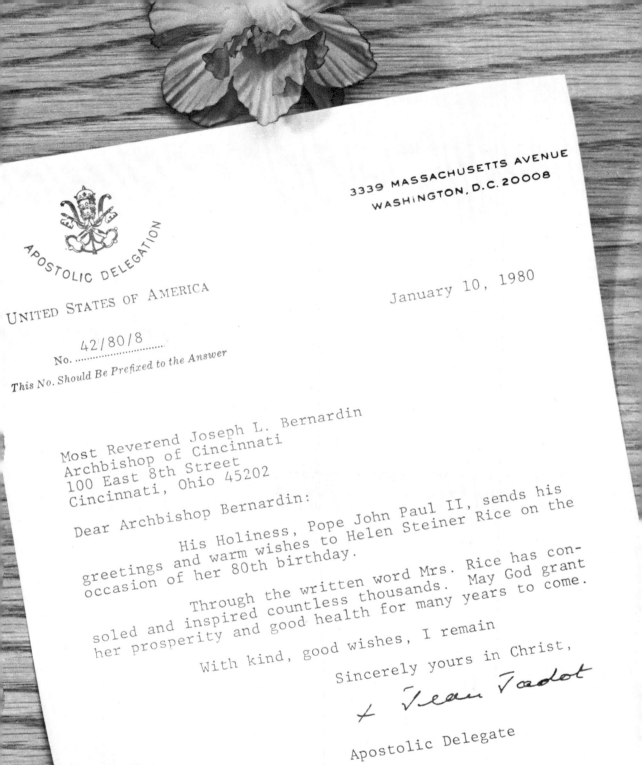

APOSTOLIC DELEGATION

UNITED STATES OF AMERICA

3339 MASSACHUSETTS AVENUE
WASHINGTON, D.C. 20008

No. 42/80/8

This No. Should Be Prefixed to the Answer

January 10, 1980

Most Reverend Joseph L. Bernardin
Archbishop of Cincinnati
100 East 8th Street
Cincinnati, Ohio 45202

Dear Archbishop Bernardin:

His Holiness, Pope John Paul II, sends his greetings and warm wishes to Helen Steiner Rice on the occasion of her 80th birthday.

Through the written word Mrs. Rice has consoled and inspired countless thousands. May God grant her prosperity and good health for many years to come.

With kind, good wishes, I remain

Sincerely yours in Christ,

+ Jean Jadot

Apostolic Delegate

DON KAUFFMAN
RR 2
SHERMAN CT 06784

western union Mailgram

4-006805S139002 05/18/80 ICS IPMMTZZ CSP CINB
2 2033551688 MGM TDMT SHERMAN CT 05-18 1239P EST

MRS HELEN STEINER RICE CARE GIBSON GREETING
CARDS
2100 SECTION RD AMBERLEY
CINCINNATI OH 45237

THIS IS A CONFIRMATION COPY OF A PREVIOUSLY PHONE-DELIVERED TELEGRAM

DEAR HELEN, YOUR WORDS ARE BLESSING MILLIONS AROUND THE WORLD. GOD
BLESS YOU EVERY MOMENT OF YOUR BIRTHDAY AND ALWAYS. LOVE
DON KAUFFMAN

12:39 EST

MGMCOMP MGM

Telegram

western union

CTB 139(0911) (4-009511S140)PD 05/19/80 0909

ICS IPMBNGZ CSP
5138416703 TDBN CINCINNATI OH 21 05-19 0909A EST

PMS HELEN STEINER RICE, DLR

ON THIS BIRTHDAY ESPECIALLY YOUR FRIENDS AND ADMIRERS AT GIBSON SEND
YOU THEIR CONGRATULATIONS, THANKS, AND WISHES FOR HEALTH AND

HAPPINESS

TOM COONEY

NNNN

THE CHRIST HOSPITAL / CINCINNATI, OHIO 45219

April 16, 1980

Mrs. Helen Steiner Rice
Gibson Greeting Cards, Inc.
2100 Section Road
Cincinnati, Ohio 45237

Dear Mrs. Rice:

What a delight to pick up the April 3 issue of The
Cincinnati Enquirer and see the lovely tribute to
you for all you have meant to so many people. It
is difficult for me to realize you are nearing
your 80th birthday. Having read so many of your
poems over the years you strike me as one of those
persons who is eternally young.

Thank you for all you have done for so many people.
Just wanted to let you know I did see the article
and rejoice and extend my congratulations on passing
that 80th milestone.

God love you,

L. H. Mayfield

L. H. Mayfield, D.D.
Director, Department of Religion

LHM:wjm

I want to be early,
No late card for me,
A good friend named Helen
Is the reason you see,
She's lovely, she's pretty,
She's talented, too,
But forget all that..
Her birthday's due,
Not her 40th or 50th, chick,
Though she's a young chick,
Not her 60th or 70th,
She's passed those sticks,
'Twill take a heap of air
To blow her candles out,
'Cause she'll have 80
Dancing flames to rout,
But knowing her the way I do,
With all her push and derring-do,
She'll turn a jig and a cartwheel, too,
Before she is completely through,
No gal of 80 has such sugar and spice,
As the one and only Helen Steiner Rice.

Happy birthday and get well.

All my love,

Fred

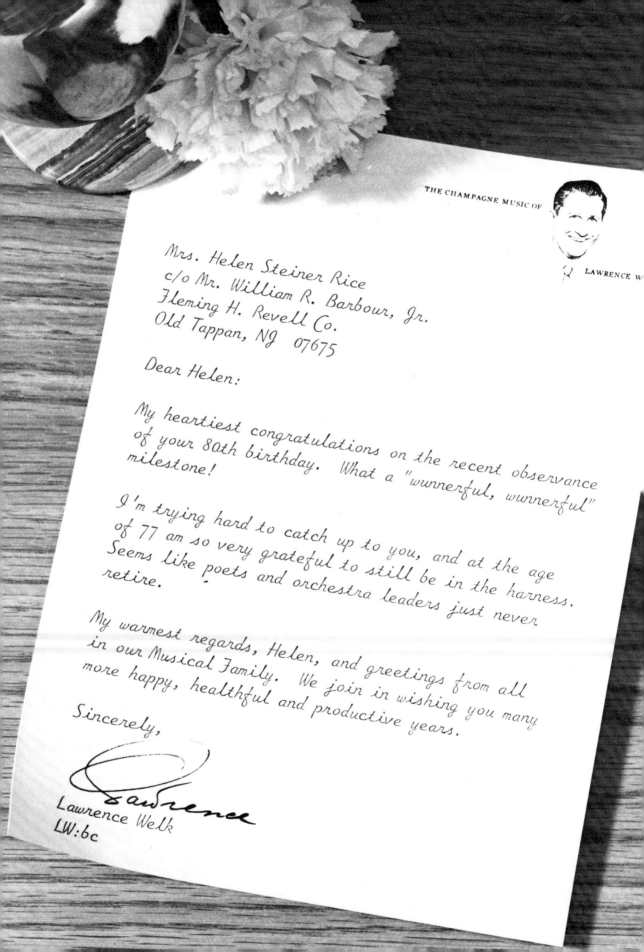

Mrs. Helen Steiner Rice
c/o Mr. William R. Barbour, Jr.
Fleming H. Revell Co.
Old Tappan, NJ 07675

Dear Helen:

My heartiest congratulations on the recent observance of your 80th birthday. What a "wunnerful, wunnerful" milestone!

I'm trying hard to catch up to you, and at the age of 77 am so very grateful to still be in the harness. Seems like poets and orchestra leaders just never retire.

My warmest regards, Helen, and greetings from all in our Musical Family. We join in wishing you many more happy, healthful and productive years.

Sincerely,

Lawrence Welk
LW:bc

City of Cincinnati
Proclamation

BE IT PROCLAIMED:

WHEREAS, Helen Steiner Rice was born on the 19th day of May, 1900, having resided in Cincinnati since 1931; and

WHEREAS, During her residency, she made notable contributions as a writer; and

WHEREAS, Her writings have uplifted, cheered and comforted people in all walks of life all over the world; and

WHEREAS, Her many humanitarian efforts and charitable contributions, though not publicized, deserve recognition; and

WHEREAS, In her 80th year she continues to make contributions to her fellow persons; and

WHEREAS, It is especially appropriate on her 80th birthday to recognize her contributions;

NOW, THEREFORE, I, J. KENNETH BLACKWELL, Mayor of the City of Cincinnati, do hereby proclaim Monday, May 19, 1980 as

HELEN STEINER RICE DAY

in Cincinnati

IN WITNESS WHEREOF, I have hereunto set my hand and caused this seal of the City of Cincinnati to be affixed this 12th day of May in the year Nineteen Hundred and Eighty.

J. Kenneth Blackwell
Mayor

God's Jewels

We watch the rich and famous
Bedecked in precious jewels,
Enjoying earthly pleasures,
Defying moral rules—
And in our mood of discontent
We sink into despair
And long for earthly riches
And feel cheated of our share—
But stop these idle musings,
God has stored up for you
Treasures that are far beyond
Earth's jewels and riches, too—
For never, never discount
What God has promised man
If he will walk in meekness
And accept God's flawless plan—
For if we heed His teachings
As we journey through the years,
We'll find the richest jewels of all
Are *crystalized* from *tears.*

The Gift of Lasting Love

Love is much more than a tender caress
    and more than bright hours of gay happiness,
For a lasting love is made up of sharing
    both hours that are "joyous" and also "despairing" . . .
It's made up of patience and deep understanding
    and never of selfish and stubborn demanding,
It's made up of "CLIMBING THE STEEP HILLS TOGETHER"
    and facing with courage "LIFE'S STORMIEST WEATHER" . . .
And nothing on earth or in heaven can part
    a love that has grown to be part of the heart,
And just like the sun and the stars and the sea,
    this love will go on through ETERNITY—
For "true love" lives on when earthly things die,
    for it's part of the SPIRIT that soars to the "SKY."

God, Grant Me the Glory of "Thy Gift"

God, widen my vision so I may see
      the afflictions You have sent to me—
Not as a CROSS too heavy to bear
      that weighs me down in gloomy despair—
Not as something to hate and despise
      but a GIFT of LOVE sent in disguise—
Something to draw me closer to You
      to teach me PATIENCE and FORBEARANCE, too—
Something to show me more clearly the way
      to SERVE You and LOVE You more every day—
Something PRICELESS and PRECIOUS and RARE
      that will keep me forever SAFE in Thy CARE
Aware of the SPIRITUAL STRENGTH that is mine
      if my selfish, small will is lost in Thine!

"The Gift of God's Love"

All over the world at this season,
Expectant hands reach to receive
Gifts that are lavishly fashioned,
The finest that man can conceive...
For, purchased and given at Christmas
Are luxuries we long to possess,
Given as favors and tokens
To try in some way to express
That strange, indefinable feeling
Which is part of this glad time of year
When streets are crowded with shoppers
And the air resounds with good cheer . . .
But back of each tinsel-tied package
Exchanged at this gift-giving season,
Unrecognized often by many,
Lies a deeper, more meaningful reason . . .
For, born in a manger at Christmas
As a gift from the Father above,
An infant whose name was called Jesus
Brought mankind the GIFT OF GOD'S LOVE . . .
And the gifts that we give have no purpose
Unless God is a part of the giving,
And unless we make Christmas a pattern
To be followed in everyday living.

Everywhere Across the Land
You See God's Face
and Touch His Hand

Each time you look up in the sky
Or watch the fluffy clouds drift by,
Or feel the sunshine warm and bright,
Or watch the dark night turn to light,
Or hear a bluebird gayly sing,
Or see the winter turn to spring,
Or stop to pick a daffodil,
Or gather violets on some hill . . .
Or touch a leaf or see a tree,
It's all *God* whispering *"This is Me . . .*
And *I am Faith* and *I am Light*
And *in Me there shall be no night."*

So Many Reasons
to Love the Lord

Thank You, God, for little things
      that come unexpectedly
To brighten up a dreary day
      that dawned so dismally—
Thank You, God, for sending
      a happy thought my way
To blot out my depression
      on a disappointing day—
Thank You, God, for brushing
      the "dark clouds" from my mind
And leaving only "sunshine"
      and joy of heart behind . . .
Oh, God, the list is endless
      of things to thank You for
But I take them all for granted
      and unconsciously ignore
That EVERYTHING I THINK or DO,
      each movement that I make,
Each measured rhythmic heartbeat,
      each breath of life I take
Is something You have given me
      for which there is no way
For me in all my "smallness"
      to in any way repay.

God Is Never
Beyond Our Reach

No one ever sought the Father
And found *He* was not *there,*
And no burden is too heavy
To be lightened by a prayer,
No problem is too intricate
And no sorrow that we face
Is too deep and devastating
To be softened by His grace,
No trials and tribulations
Are beyond what we can bear
If we share them with *Our Father*
As we talk to *Him* in prayer—
And men of every color,
Every race and every creed
Have but to seek the Father
In their deepest hour of need—
God asks for no credentials,
He accepts us with our flaws,
He is kind and understanding
And He welcomes us because
We are His erring children
And He loves us everyone,
And He freely and completely
Forgives all that we have done,
Asking only if we're ready
To follow *where He leads*—
Content that in His wisdom
He will answer all our needs.

Unaware, We Pass "Him" By

On life's busy thoroughfares
We meet with *angels* unawares—
But we are too busy to listen or hear,
Too busy to sense that God is near,
Too busy to stop and recognize
The grief that lies in another's eyes,
Too busy to offer to help or share,
Too busy to sympathize or care,
Too busy to do the *good things* we should,
Telling ourselves we would if we could . . .
But life is too swift and the pace is too great
And we dare not pause for we might be late
For our next appointment which means so much,
We are willing to brush off the Saviour's touch,
And we tell ourselves there will come a day
We will have more time to pause on our way . . .
But before we know it "life's sun has set"
And we've passed the Saviour but never met,
For hurrying along life's thoroughfare
We passed Him by and remained unaware
That within the *very sight of our eye,*
Unnoticed, the Son of God passed by.

Anywhere Is a Place of Prayer
If God Is There

I have prayed on my knees in the morning,
I have prayed as I walked along,
I have prayed in the silence and darkness
And I've prayed to the tune of a song—
I have prayed in the midst of triumph
And I've prayed when I suffered defeat,
I have prayed on the sands of the seashore
Where the waves of the ocean beat—
I have prayed in a velvet-hushed forest
Where the quietness calmed my fears,
I have prayed through suffering and heartache
When my eyes were blinded with tears—
I have prayed in churches and chapels,
Cathedrals and synagogues, too,
But often I've had the feeling
That my prayers were not getting through,
And I realized then that our Father
Is not really concerned where we pray
Or impressed by our manner of worship
Or the eloquent words that we say . . .
He is only concerned with our feelings,
And He looks deep into our heart
And hears the "cry of our soul's deep need"
That no words could ever impart . . .
So it isn't the prayer that's expressive
Or offered in some special spot,
It's the sincere plea of a sinner
And God can tell whether or not
We honestly seek His forgiveness
And earnestly mean what we say,
And then and then only He answers
The prayer that we fervently pray.

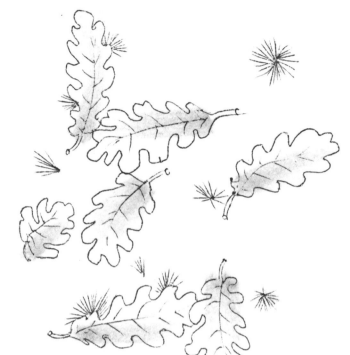

Where Can We Find Him?

Where can we find *the Holy One?*
Where can we see *His Only Son?*
The Wise Men asked, and we're asking still,
Where Can We Find This Man of Good
    Will?
Is He far away in some distant place,
Ruling unseen from His throne of grace?
Is there nothing on earth that man can see
To give him proof of *Eternity?*
It's true we have never looked on His face,
But His likeness shines forth from every place,
For *The Hand of God* is everywhere
Along life's busy thoroughfare . . .
And His presence can be felt and seen
Right in the midst of our daily routine,
The things we touch and see and feel
Are what make God so very real . . .
The silent stars in timeless skies,
The wonderment in children's eyes,
The gossamer wings of a humming bird,
The joy that comes from a kindly word . . .
The autumn haze, the breath of spring,
The chirping song the crickets sing,

A rosebud in a slender vase,
A smile upon a friendly face . . .
In everything both great and small
We see *the Hand of God in All,*
And every day, somewhere, someplace,
We see *the Likeness of His Face* . . .
For who can watch a new day's birth
Or touch the warm, life-giving earth,
Or feel the softness of the breeze
Or look at skies through lacy trees
And say they've never seen His face
Or looked upon His throne of grace!

In Hours of Discouragement
God Is Our Encouragement

Sometimes we feel uncertain
And unsure of everything,
Afraid to make decisions,
Dreading what the day will bring—
We keep wishing it were possible
To dispel all fear and doubt
And to understand more readily
Just what life is all about—
God has given us the answers
Which too often go unheeded,
But if we search His promises
We'll find everything that's needed
To lift our faltering spirits
And renew our courage, too,
For there's absolutely nothing
Too much for God to do—
For the Lord is our salvation
And our strength in every fight,
Our redeemer and protector,
Our eternal guiding light—
He has promised to sustain us,
He's our refuge from all harms,

And underneath this refuge
Are the everlasting arms—
So cast your burden on Him,
Seek His counsel when distressed,
And go to Him for comfort
When you're lonely and oppressed—
For God is our encouragement
In trouble and in trials,
And in suffering and in sorrow
He will turn our tears to smiles.

Love: God's Gift Divine

Love is enduring
And patient and kind,
It judges all things
With the heart not the mind,
And love can transform
The most commonplace
Into beauty and splendor
And sweetness and grace . . .
For love is unselfish,
Giving more than it takes,
And no matter what happens
Love never forsakes,
It's faithful and trusting
And always believing,
Guileless and honest
And never deceiving . . .
Yes, love is beyond
What man can define,
For love is immortal
And God's Gift is Divine!

The Priceless Gift

The priceless gift of life is love,
For with the help of God above
Love can change the human race
And make this world a better place—
For love dissolves all hate and fear
And makes our vision bright and clear
So we can see and rise above
Our pettiness on "wings of love."

The Gift of Friendship

Friendship is a priceless gift
That cannot be bought or sold,
But its value is far greater
Than a mountain made of gold—
For gold is cold and lifeless,
It can neither see nor hear,
And in the time of trouble
It is powerless to cheer—
It has no ears to listen,
No heart to understand,
It cannot bring you comfort
Or reach out a helping hand—
So when you ask God for a Gift,
Be thankful if He sends
Not diamonds, pearls or riches,
But the love of real true friends.

A Friend Is a Gift of God

Among the great and glorious gifts
      our heavenly Father sends
Is the GIFT of UNDERSTANDING
      that we find in loving friends,
For in this world of trouble
      that is filled with anxious care
Everybody needs a friend
      in whom they're free to share
The little secret heartaches
      that lay heavy on their mind,
Not just a mere acquaintance
      but someone who's "JUST OUR KIND"—
For, somehow, in the generous heart
      of loving, faithful friends
The good God in His charity
      and wisdom always sends
A sense of understanding
      and the power of perception
And mixes these fine qualities
      with kindness and affection
So when we need some sympathy
      or a friendly hand to touch,
Or an ear that listens tenderly
      and speaks words that mean so much,
We seek our true and trusted friend
      in the knowledge that we'll find
A heart that's sympathetic
      and an understanding mind . . .
And often just without a word
      there seems to be a union
Of thoughts and kindred feelings
      for GOD gives TRUE FRIENDS communion.

Blessings in Disguise
Are Difficult to Recognize

God sends His "little angels"
      in many forms and guises,
They come as lovely miracles
      that God alone devises—
For He does nothing without purpose,
      everything's a perfect plan
To fulfill in bounteous measure
      all He ever promised man—
For every "little angel"
      with a body bent and broken,
Or a little mind retarded
      or little words unspoken,
Is just God's way of trying
      to reach and touch the hand
Of all who do not know Him
      and cannot understand
That often through an angel
      whose "wings will never fly"
The Lord is pointing out the way
      to His eternal sky
Where there will be no handicaps
      of body, soul or mind,
And where all limitations
      will be dropped and left behind—
So accept these "little angels"
      as gifts from God above
And thank Him for this lesson
      in *Faith* and *Hope* and *Love.*

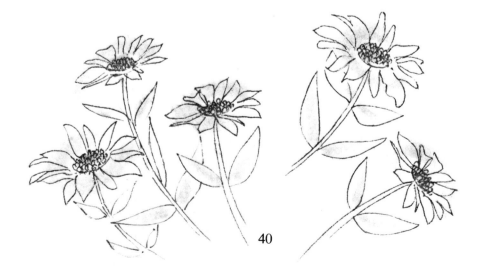

Before You Can Dry Another's Tears—
You Too Must Weep!

Let me not live a life that's free
From *"the things"* that draw me close to *Thee*—
For how can I ever hope to heal
The wounds of others I do not feel—
If my eyes are dry and I never weep,
How do I know when the hurt is deep—
If my heart is cold and it never bleeds,
How can I tell what my brother needs—
For when ears are deaf to the beggar's plea
And we close our eyes and refuse to see,
And we steel our hearts and harden our mind,
And we count it a weakness whenever we're kind,
We are no longer following *the Father's Way*
Or seeking His guidance from day to day—
For, without "crosses to carry" and "burdens to bear,"
We dance through a life that is frothy and fair,
And "chasing the rainbow" we have no desire
For "roads that are rough" and "realms that are higher"—
So spare me no heartache or sorrow, dear Lord,
For the heart that is hurt reaps the richest reward,
And God enters the heart that is broken with sorrow
As He opens the door to a *Brighter Tomorrow*,
For only through tears can we recognize
The suffering that lies in another's eyes.

Trouble Is a Stepping-Stone to Growth

Trouble is something no one can escape,
Everyone has it in some form or shape—
Some people hide it way down deep inside,
Some people bear it with gallant-like pride,
Some people worry and complain of their lot,
Some people covet what they haven't got,
While others rebel and become bitter and old
With hopes that are dead and hearts that are cold . . .
But the wise man accepts whatever God sends,
Willing to yield like a storm-tossed tree bends,
Knowing that God never makes a mistake,
So whatever He sends they are willing to take—
For trouble is part and parcel of life
And no man can grow without trouble and strife,
And the steep hills ahead and high mountain peaks
Afford man at last the peace that he seeks—
So blest are the people who learn to accept
The trouble men try to escape and reject,
For in *our acceptance*
　　　we're given great grace
And courage and faith and the strength to face
The daily troubles that come to us all
So we may learn to stand "straight and tall"—
For the grandeur of life is born of defeat
For in overcoming we make life complete.

When Trouble Comes
and Things Go Wrong!

Let us go quietly to God
      when troubles come to us,
Let us never stop to whimper
      or complain and fret and fuss,
Let us hide "our thorns" in "roses"
      and our sighs in "golden song"
And "our crosses" in a "crown of smiles"
      whenever things go wrong . . .
For no one can really help us
      as our troubles we bemoan,
For *comfort, help* and *inner peace*
      must come from God alone . . .
So do not tell your neighbor,
      your companion or your friend
In the hope that they can help you
      bring your troubles to an end . . .
For they, too, have their problems,
      they are burdened just like you,
So *take your cross to Jesus*
      and *He will see you through* . . .
And waste no time in crying
      on the shoulder of a friend
But go directly to the Lord
      for on Him you can depend . . .
For there's absolutely *nothing*
      that His mighty hand can't do
And He never is too busy
      to help and comfort you.

God Knows Best

Our Father knows what's best for us,
So why should we complain—
We always want the sunshine
But He knows there must be rain—
We love the sound of laughter
And the merriment of cheer,
But our hearts would lose their tenderness
If we never shed a tear . . .
Our Father tests us often
With suffering and with sorrow,
He tests us, not to punish us,
But to help us meet *tomorrow* . . .
For growing trees are strengthened
When they withstand the storm,
And the sharp cut of the chisel
Gives the marble grace and form . . .
God never hurts us needlessly,
And He never wastes our pain,
For every loss He sends to us
Is followed by rich gain . . .
And when we count the blessings
That God has so freely sent,
We will find no cause for murmuring
And no time to lament . . .
For Our Father loves His children,
And to Him all things are plain,
So He never sends us *pleasure*
When the *soul's deep need is pain* . . .
So whenever we are troubled,
And when everything goes wrong,
It is just God working in us
To make *our spirit strong.*

"This Too Will Pass Away"

If I can endure for this minute
Whatever is happening to me,
No matter how heavy my heart is
Or how "dark" the moment may be—
If I can remain calm and quiet
With all my world crashing about me,
Secure in the knowledge God loves me
When everyone else seems to doubt me—
If I can but keep on believing
What I know in my heart to be true,
That "darkness will fade with the morning"
And that *this will pass away, too*—
Then nothing in life can defeat me
For as long as this knowledge remains
I can suffer whatever is happening
For I know God will break "all the chains"
That are binding me tight in *"the Darkness"*
And trying to fill me with fear—
For there is *no night without dawning*
And I know that *"my morning"* is near.

Quit Supposin'

Don't start your day by supposin'
     that trouble is just ahead,
It's better to stop supposin'
     and start with a prayer instead,
And make it a prayer of *Thanksgiving*
     for the wonderful things God has wrought
Like the beautiful sunrise and sunset,
     "God's Gifts" that are free
     and not bought—
For what is the use of supposin'
     the dire things that could happen to you
And worry about some misfortune
     that seldom if ever comes true—
But instead of just idle supposin'
     step forward to meet each new day
Secure in the knowledge God's near you
     to lead you each step of the way—
For supposin' the worst things will happen
     only helps to make them come true
And you darken the bright, happy moments
     that the dear Lord has given to you—
So if you desire to be happy
     and get rid of the *"misery of dread"*
Just give up *"Supposin' the worst things"*
     and look for *"the best things"* instead.

Never Borrow Sorrow
From Tomorrow

Deal only with the present,
Never step into tomorrow,
For God asks us just to trust Him
And to never borrow sorrow—
For the future is not ours to know
And, it may never be,
So let us live and give our best
And give it lavishly—
For to meet tomorrow's troubles
Before they are even ours
Is to anticipate the Saviour
And to doubt His all-wise powers—
So let us be content to solve
Our problems one by one,
Asking nothing of tomorrow
Except *"Thy Will be done."*

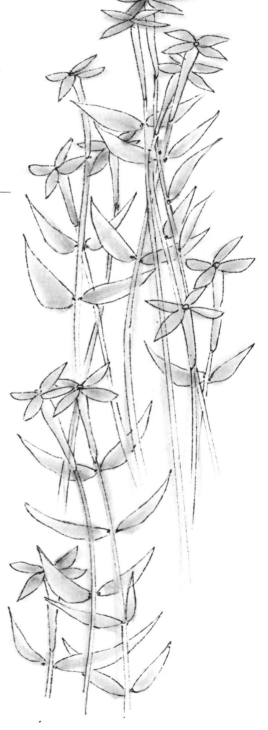

A Sure Way to a Happy Day

Happiness is something
      we create in our mind,
It's not something you search for
      and so seldom find—
It's just waking up
      and beginning the day
By counting our blessings
      and kneeling to pray—
It's giving up thoughts
      that breed discontent
And accepting what comes
      as a "gift heaven-sent"—
It's giving up wishing
      for things we have not
And making the best of
      whatever we've got—
It's knowing that life
      is determined for us,
And pursuing our tasks
      without fret, fume or fuss—
For it's by completing
      what God gives us to do
That we find real contentment
      and happiness, too.

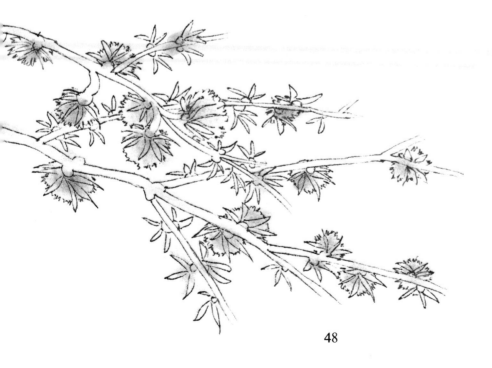

Prayers Are the Stairs to God

Prayers are the stairs
We must climb every day,
If we would reach God
There is no other way,
For we learn to know God
When we meet Him in prayer
And ask Him to lighten
Our burden of care—
So start in the morning
And, though the way's steep,
Climb ever upward
'Til your eyes close in sleep—
For prayers are the stairs
That lead to the Lord,
And to meet Him in prayer
Is the climber's reward.

No Prayer Goes Unheard

Often we pause and wonder
When we kneel down to pray—
Can God really hear
The prayers that we say . . .
But if we keep praying
And talking to *Him,*
He'll brighten the soul
That was clouded and dim,
And as we continue
Our burden seems lighter,
Our sorrow is softened
And our outlook is brighter—
For though we feel helpless
And alone when we start,
Our prayer is the key
That opens the heart,
And as our heart opens
The dear Lord comes in
And the prayer that we felt
We could never begin
Is so easy to say
For the Lord understands
And gives us new strength
By the touch of His hands.

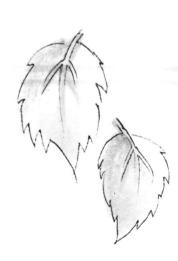

Prayers Can't Be Answered
Unless They Are Prayed

Life without purpose
        is barren indeed—
There can't be a harvest
        unless you plant seed,
There can't be attainment
        unless there's a goal,
And man's but a robot
        unless there's a soul . . .
If we send no ships out,
        no ships will come in,
And unless there's a contest,
        nobody can win . . .
For games can't be won
        unless they are played,
And *Prayers* can't be *answered*
        unless they are *prayed* . . .
So whatever is wrong
        with your life today,
You'll find a solution
        if you kneel down and pray
Not just for pleasure,
        enjoyment and health,
Not just for honors
        and prestige and wealth . . .
But *Pray for a Purpose*
        to *make life worth living,*
And *Pray for the Joy*
        of *unselfish giving,*
For *Great is your Gladness*
        and *Rich your Reward*
When you make your *Life's Purpose*
        the choice of the Lord.

Daily Prayers Dissolve Your Cares

I meet God in the morning
And go with Him through the day,
Then in the stillness of the night
Before sleep comes I pray
That God will just "take over"
All the problems I couldn't solve
And in the peacefulness of sleep
My cares will all dissolve,
So when I open up my eyes
To greet another day
I'll find myself renewed in strength
And there'll open up a way
To meet what seemed impossible
For me to solve alone
And once again I'll be assured
I am never *"on my own"* . . .
For if we try to stand alone
We are weak and we will fall,
For God is always *Greatest*
When we're helpless, lost and small,
And no day is unmeetable
If on rising our first thought
Is to thank God for the blessings
That His loving care has brought . . .

For there can be no failures
Or hopeless, unsaved sinners
If we enlist the help of God
Who makes all losers winners . . .
So meet Him in the morning
And go with Him through the day
And thank Him for His guidance
Each evening when you pray,
And if you follow faithfully
This daily way to pray
You will never in your lifetime
Face another "hopeless day."

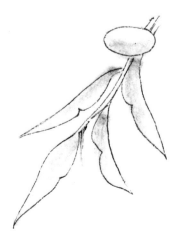

The Magic of Love

LOVE is like MAGIC
And it always will be,
For love still remains
LIFE'S SWEET MYSTERY!

LOVE works in ways
That are wondrous and strange
And there's NOTHING IN LIFE
That LOVE CANNOT CHANGE!

LOVE can transform
The most commonplace
Into beauty and splendor
And sweetness and grace!

LOVE is unselfish,
Understanding and kind,
For it sees with its HEART
And not with its mind!

LOVE is the answer
That everyone seeks—
LOVE is the language
That every heart speaks—

LOVE can't be bought,
It is priceless and free,
LOVE like pure MAGIC
Is a SWEET MYSTERY!

God's Love

GOD'S LOVE is like an island
In life's ocean vast and wide—
A peaceful, quiet shelter
From the restless, rising tide . . .

GOD'S LOVE is like an anchor
When the angry billows roll—
A mooring in the storms of life,
A stronghold for the soul . . .

GOD'S LOVE is like a fortress
And we seek protection there
When the waves of tribulation
Seem to drown us in despair . . .

GOD'S LOVE is like a harbor
Where our souls can find sweet rest
From the struggle and the tension
Of life's fast and futile quest . . .

GOD'S LOVE is like a beacon
Burning bright with FAITH and PRAYER
And through the changing scenes of life
We can find a HAVEN THERE!

God, Grant Us Hope
and Faith and Love

HOPE for a world
      grown cynically cold,
Hungry for power
      and greedy for gold . . .

FAITH to believe
      when within and without
There's a nameless fear
      in a world of doubt . . .

LOVE that is bigger
      than race or creed,
To cover the world
      and fulfill each need . . .

      GOD, GRANT THESE GIFTS
      Of FAITH, HOPE and LOVE—
      Three things this world
      Has so little of . . .
      For only THESE GIFTS
      From OUR FATHER ABOVE
      Can turn man's sins
      From HATRED to LOVE!

Warm Our Hearts With Thy Love

Oh, God, who made the summer
     and warmed the earth with beauty,
Warm our hearts with gratitude
     and devotion to our duty,
For in this age of violence,
     rebellion and defiance
We've forgotten the true meaning
     of "dependable reliance"—
We have lost our sense of duty
     and our sense of values, too,
And what was once unsanctioned,
     no longer is taboo,
Our standards have been lowered
     and we resist all discipline,
And our vision has been narrowed
     and blinded to all sin—
Oh, put the summer brightness
     in our closed, unseeing eyes
So in the careworn faces
     that we pass we'll recognize
The heartbreak and the loneliness,
     the trouble and despair
That a word of understanding
     would make easier to bear—
Oh, God, look down on our cold hearts
     and warm them with Your love,
And grant us Your forgiveness
     which we're so unworthy of.

In the Garden of Gethsemane

Before the dawn of Easter
     There came Gethsemane . . .
Before the Resurrection
     There were hours of agony . . .
For there can be no crown of stars
     Without a cross to bear,
And there is no salvation
     Without *Faith* and *Love* and *Prayer,*
And when we take our needs to God
     Let us pray as did His Son
That dark night in Gethsemane—
     "Thy Will, Not Mine, Be Done."

"Why Should He Die for Such as I"

In everything both great and small
We see the Hand of God in all,
And in the miracles of Spring
When *everywhere* in *everything*
His handiwork is all around
And every lovely sight and sound
Proclaims the God of earth and sky
I ask myself *"Just Who Am I"*
That God should send His only Son
That my salvation would be won
Upon a *cross* by a sinless man
To bring fulfillment to God's Plan—
For Jesus suffered, bled and died
That sinners might be sanctified,
And to grant God's children *such as I*
Eternal life in that *Home* on *High.*

My God Is No Stranger

I've never seen God,
        but I know how I feel . . .
It's people like *you*
        who make *Him "so real"* . . .
My God is no stranger,
        He's friendly and gay . . .
And *He* doesn't ask me
        to weep when I pray . . .
It seems that I pass *Him*
        so often each day . . .
In the faces of people
        I meet on my way . . .
He's the stars in the heaven,
        a smile on some face . . .
A leaf on a tree
        or a rose in a vase . . .
He's winter and autumn
        and summer and spring . . .
In short, *God is Every*
        Real, Wonderful Thing . . .
I wish I might meet *Him*
        much more than I do . . .
I would if there were
        more people like you.

Widen My Vision

God open my eyes
    so I may see
And feel Your presence
    close to me . . .
Give me strength
    for my stumbling feet
As I battle the crowd
    on life's busy street,
And widen the vision
    of my unseeing eyes
So in passing faces
    I'll recognize
Not just a stranger,
    unloved and unknown,
But a friend with a heart
    that is much like my own . . .
Give me perception
    to make me aware
That scattered profusely
    on life's thoroughfare
Are the best *Gifts of God*
    that we daily pass by
As we look at the world
    with an *unseeing eye.*

"I Know That My Redeemer Liveth"

They asked me how I know it's true
That the Saviour lived and died . . .
And if I believe the story
That the Lord was crucified?
And I have so many answers
To prove His Holy Being,
Answers that are everywhere
Within the realm of seeing . . .
The leaves that fell at autumn
And were buried in the sod
Now budding on the tree boughs
To lift their arms to God . . .
The flowers that were covered
And entombed beneath the snow
Pushing through the "darkness"
To bid the Spring "hello" . . .
On every side Great Nature
Retells the Easter Story—
So who am I to question
"The Resurrection Glory"?

"I Am the Light of the World"

Oh Father, up in heaven,
      We have wandered far away
From Jesus Christ, Our Saviour,
      Who arose on Easter Day . . .
And the promise of salvation
      That God gave us when Christ died
We have often vaguely questioned,
      Even doubted and denied . . .
We've forgotten why You sent us
      Jesus Christ Your Only Son,
And in arrogance and ignorance—
      It's *Our Will,* not *Thine, Be Done* . . .
Oh, shed *Thy Light* upon us
      As Easter dawns this year,
And may we feel *The Presence*
      Of the *Risen Saviour* near . . .
And, God, in Thy great wisdom,
      Lead us in the way that's right,
And may *"The Darkness"* of this world
      Be conquered by *"Thy Light."*

More of Thee . . . Less of Me

Take me and break me and make me, dear God,
Just what you want me to be—
Give me the strength to accept what you send
And eyes with the vision to see
All the small arrogant ways that I have
And the vain little things that I do,
Make me aware that I'm often concerned
More with *myself* than with *You,*
Uncover before me my weakness and greed
And help me to search deep inside
So I may discover how easy it is
To be selfishly lost in my pride—
And then in Thy goodness and mercy
Look down on this weak, erring one
And tell me that I am forgiven
For all I've so willfully done,
And teach me to humbly start following
The path that the dear Saviour trod
So I'll find at the end of life's journey
"A Home in the city of God."

God, Give Us "Drive" but Keep Us From Being "Driven"

There's a difference between "drive" and "driven"—
The one is selfish the other God-given—
For the "driven man" has but one goal,
Just worldly wealth and not "riches of soul,"
And daily he's spurred on to reach and attain
A higher position, more profit and gain,
Ambition and wealth become his great need
As daily he's "driven" by avarice and greed . . .
But most blessed are they who use their "drive"
To work with zeal so all men may survive,
For while they forfeit great personal gain
Their work and their zeal are never in vain . . .
For they contribute to the whole human race
And we cannot survive without growing in grace,
So help us, dear God, to choose between
The "driving force" that rules our routine
So we may make our purpose and goal
Not power and wealth but the growth of our soul . . .
And give us *strength* and *drive* and *desire*
To raise our standards and ethics higher
So all of Us and not *just a few*
May live on earth . . . *as You want Us to.*

The Way to God

If my days were untroubled
    and my heart always light
Would I seek that fair land
    where there is no night;
If I never grew weary
    with the weight of my load
Would I search for God's Peace
    at the end of the road;
If I never knew sickness
    and never felt pain
Would I reach for a hand
    to help and sustain;
If I walked not with sorrow
    and lived without loss
Would my soul seek sweet solace
    at the foot of the cross;
If all I desired was mine
    day by day
Would I kneel before God
    and earnestly pray;

If God sent no "Winter"
     to freeze me with fear
Would I yearn for the warmth
     of "Spring" every year;
I ask myself this
     and the answer is plain—
If my life were all pleasure
     and I never knew pain
I'd seek God less often
     and need Him much less,
For God's sought more often
     in times of distress,
And no one knows God
     or sees Him as plain
As those who have met Him
     on "The Pathway of Pain."

The World Would Be
a Nicer Place If We
Traveled at a Slower Pace

Amid stresses and strains
much too many to mention,
And pressure-packed days
filled with turmoil and tension,
We seldom have time
to be "Friendly or Kind"
For we're harassed and hurried
and always behind—
And while we've more "gadgets"
and "buttons to press"
Making leisure hours greater
and laboring hours less,
And our standards of living
they claim have improved
And "repressed inhibitions"
have been freed and removed,
It seems all this Progress
and Growth are for naught,
For daily we see a World More Distraught—
So what does it matter
if man reaches his goal
"And gains the whole world but loses his soul"—
For what have we won
if in gaining this end
We've been much too busy
to be Kind To A Friend,
And what is there left to make the heart sing
When life is a Cold and Mechanical Thing
And we are but puppets
of controlled automation
Instead of "joint heirs"
to "God's Gift Of Creation."

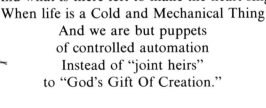

Faith Is a Mighty Fortress

We stand once more at the end of the year
With mixed emotions of *hope and fear,*
Hope for *the Peace* we long have sought,
Fear that *our hopes* will come to naught . . .
Unwilling to trust in the *Father's Will,*
We count on our logic and shallow skill
And, in our arrogance and pride,
Man is no longer satisfied
To place his confidence and love
With *Childlike Faith* in God above . . .
But tiny hands and tousled heads
That kneel in prayer by little beds
Are closer to the dear Lord's heart
And of His Kingdom more a part
Than we who search and never find
The answers to our questioning mind,
For faith in things we cannot see
Requires a child's simplicity . . .
Oh, Father, grant once more to men
A simple *Childlike Faith* again,
Forgetting *color, race* and *creed*
And seeing only the heart's deep need . . .
For *Faith* alone can save man's soul
And lead him to a *higher goal,*
For there's but one unfailing course—
We win by *Faith* and *not* by *Force.*

A Prayer for Patience

God, teach me to be patient—
Teach me to go slow—
Teach me how to "wait on You"
When my way I do not know . . .
Teach me sweet forbearance
When things do not go right
So I remain unruffled
When others grow uptight . . .
Teach me how to quiet
My racing, rising heart
So I may hear the answer
You are trying to impart . . .
Teach me to LET GO, dear God,
And pray undisturbed until
My heart is filled with inner peace
And I learn to know YOUR WILL!

Time Is a Gift of God

We stand once more
on the threshold
of a shining and unblemished year,
Untouched yet by *Time* and *Frustration*,
unclouded by *Failure* and *Fear* . . .
How will we use the days of this year
and the *Time* God has placed in our hands,
Will we waste the minutes
and squander the hours,
leaving "no prints behind in time's sands" . . .
Will we vainly complain
that *Life* is *So Swift*,
that we haven't the *Time to Do Good*,
Our days are too crowded,
our hours are too short
to do *All the Good Things* we should . . .
We say we would pray
if we just had the time,
and be kind to all those in need,
But we live in a world
of *"Planned Progress"*
and our national password is *"Speed"* . . .
God, grant us the grace
as another year starts
to use all the hours of our days,
Not for our own selfish interests
and our own willful, often-wrong ways . . .
But teach us
to *Take Time for Praying*
and to find time
for *Listening to You*
So each day is spent
well and wisely
doing *What You Most Want Us to Do.*

The Praying Hands

The *"Praying Hands"* are much, much more
than just a work of art,
They are the "soul's creation"
of a deeply thankful heart—
They are a *Priceless Masterpiece*
that love alone could paint,
And they reveal the selflessness
of an unheralded saint—
These hands so scarred and toilworn,
tell the story of a man
Who sacrificed his talent
in accordance with God's Plan—
For in God's Plan are many things
man cannot understand,
But we must trust God's judgment
and be guided by His Hand—
Sometimes He asks us to give up
our dreams of happiness,
Sometimes we must forego our hopes
of fortune and success—
Not all of us can triumph

or rise to heights of fame,
And many times *What Should Be Ours,*
goes to *Another Name*—
But he who makes a sacrifice,
so another may succeed,
Is indeed a true disciple
of our blessed Saviour's creed—
For when we "give ourselves away"
in sacrifice and love,
We are "laying up rich treasures"
in God's kingdom up above—
And hidden in gnarled, toilworn hands
is the truest *Art of Living,*
Achieved alone by those who've learned
the *"Victory of Giving"*—
For any sacrifice on earth,
made in the dear Lord's name,
Assures the giver of a place
in *Heaven's Hall of Fame*—
And who can say with certainty
Where the Greatest Talent Lies,
Or Who Will Be the Greatest
In Our Heavenly Father's Eyes!

The Peace of Meditation

So we may know God better
And feel His quiet power,
Let us daily keep in silence
A *meditation hour*—
For to understand God's greatness
And to use His gifts each day
The soul must learn to meet Him
In a meditative way,
For our Father tells His children
That if they would know His will
They must seek Him in the silence
When all is calm and still . . .
For nature's greatest forces
Are found in quiet things
Like softly falling snowflakes
Drifting down on angels' wings,
Or petals dropping soundlessly
From a lovely full-blown rose,
So God comes closest to us
When our souls are in repose . . .
So let us plan with prayerful care
To always allocate
A certain portion of each day
To be still and meditate . . .
For when everything is quiet

And we're lost in meditation,
Our soul is then preparing
For a deeper dedication
That will make it wholly possible
To quietly endure
The violent world around us—
For in God we are secure.

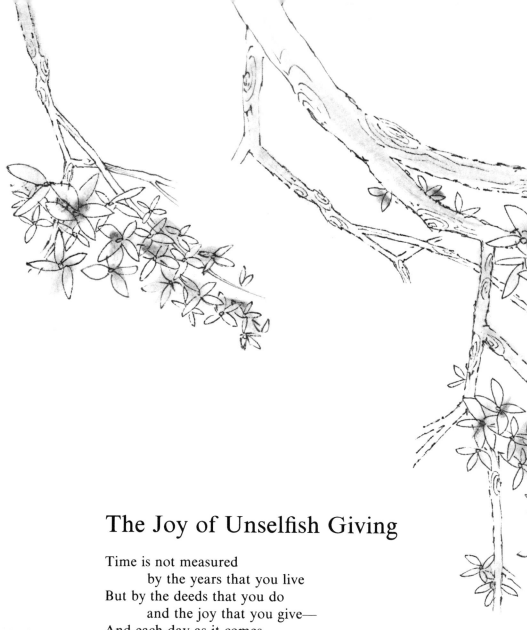

The Joy of Unselfish Giving

Time is not measured
        by the years that you live
But by the deeds that you do
        and the joy that you give—
And each day as it comes
        brings a chance to each one
To love to the fullest,
        leaving nothing undone
That would brighten the life
        or lighten the load
Of some weary traveler
        lost on Life's Road—
So what does it matter
        how long we may live
If as long as we live
        we unselfishly give.

Every Day Is a Reason
for Giving—and
Giving Is the Key to Living!

So let us give "ourselves" away
Not just today but every day . . .
And remember a kind and thoughtful deed
Or a hand outstretched in time of need
Is the rarest of gifts, for it is a part
Not of the purse but a loving heart—
And he who gives of himself will find
True joy of heart and peace of mind.

Give Lavishly! Live Abundantly!

The more you give, the more you get—
The more you laugh, the less you fret—
The more you do *unselfishly,*
The more you live *abundantly* . . .

The more of everything you share,
The more you'll always have to spare—
The more you love, the more you'll find
That life is good and friends are kind . . .

For only *what we give away,*
Enriches us from day to day.

Not by the Years We Live
but How Much We Give

From one day to another
      GOD will gladly give
To everyone who seeks HIM
      and tries each day to live
A little bit more closely
      to GOD and to each other,
Seeing everyone who passes
      as a neighbor, friend, or brother,
Not only joy and happiness
      but the faith to meet each trial
Not with fear and trepidation
      but with an "inner smile"—
For we know life's never measured
      by how many years we live
But by the kindly things we do
      and the happiness we give.

The Seasons of the Soul

Why am I cast down
  and despondently sad
When I long to be happy
  and joyous and glad?
Why is my heart heavy
  with unfathomable weight
As I try to escape
  this soul-saddened state?
I ask myself often—
  "What makes life this way,
Why is the song silenced
  in the heart that was gay?"
And then with God's help
  it all becomes clear,
The *Soul* has its *Seasons*
  just the same as the year—
I too must pass through
  life's autumn of dying,
A desolate period
  of heart-hurt and crying,
Followed by winter
  in whose frostbitten hand
My heart is as frozen
  as the snow-covered land—
Yes, man too must pass
  through the seasons God sends,

Content in the knowledge
        that everything ends,
And oh what a blessing
        to know there are reasons
And to find that our soul
        must, too, have its seasons—
Bounteous Seasons
        and *Barren Ones,* too,
Times for rejoicing
        and times to be blue,
But meeting these seasons
        of dark desolation
With strength that is born
        of anticipation
That comes from knowing
        that "autumn-time sadness"
Will surely be followed
        by a "Springtime of Gladness."

The Priceless Gift of Christmas

Now Christmas is a season
    for joy and merrymaking,
A time for gifts and presents,
    for giving and for taking . . .
A festive, friendly happy time
    when everyone is gay—
But have we ever really felt
    the *greatness of the day* . . .
For through the centuries the world
    has wandered far away
From the beauty and the meaning
    of the *Holy Christmas Day* . . .
For Christmas is a heavenly gift
    that only God can give,
It's ours just for the asking,
    for as long as we shall live . . .
It can't be bought or bartered,
    it can't be won or sold,
It doesn't cost a penny
    and it's worth far more than gold . . .
It isn't bright and gleaming
    for eager eyes to see,
It can't be wrapped in tinsel
    or placed beneath a tree . . .
It isn't soft and shimmering
    for reaching hands to touch,

Or some expensive luxury
        you've wanted very much . . .
For the *priceless Gift of Christmas*
        is meant just for the heart
And we receive it only
        when we become a part
Of the kingdom and the glory
        which is ours to freely take,
For God sent the Holy Christ Child
        at Christmas for our sake,
So man might come to know *Him*
        and feel *His Presence* near
And see the many miracles
        performed while *He* was here . . .
And this *priceless Gift of Christmas*
        is within the reach of all,
The rich, the poor, the young and old
        the greatest and the small . . .
So take *His Priceless Gift of Love,*
        reach out and you receive,
And the only payment that God asks
        is just that *you believe.*

Let Us Pray on This Holy Christmas Day

What better time
And what better season,
What greater occasion
Or more wonderful reason
To kneel down in prayer
And lift our hands high
To the God of creation
Who made land and sky . . .
And, oh, what a privilege
As the New Year begins
To ask God to wipe out
Our errors and sins
And to know when we ask,
If we are sincere,
He will wipe our slate clean
As we start a New Year . . .
So at this glad season
When joy's everywhere,
Let us meet Our Redeemer
At the *Altar* of *Prayer*.

After the Winter . . .
God Sends the Spring

Springtime is a season
    Of Hope and Joy and Cheer,
There's beauty all around us
    To see and touch and hear . . .
So, no matter how downhearted
    And discouraged we may be,
New Hope is born when we behold
    Leaves budding on a tree . . .
Or when we see a timid flower
    Push through the frozen sod
And open wide in glad surprise
    Its petaled eyes to God . . .
For this is just God saying—
    "Lift up your eyes to Me,
And the bleakness of your spirit,
    Like the budding springtime tree,
Will lose its wintry darkness
    And your heavy heart will sing"—
For God never sends The Winter
    Without the Joy of Spring.

Spring Song

"The earth is the Lord's
     and the fulness thereof"—
It speaks of His greatness
     and it sings of His love,
And the wonder and glory
     of the first Easter morn,
Like the first Christmas night
     when the Saviour was born,
Are blended together
     in symphonic splendor
And God with a voice
     that is gentle and tender
Speaks to all hearts
     attuned to His voice,
Bidding His listeners
     to gladly rejoice . . .
For He who was born
     to be crucified
Arose from the grave
     to be glorified . . .
And the birds in the trees
     and the flowers of Spring
All join in proclaiming
     this heavenly King.

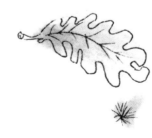

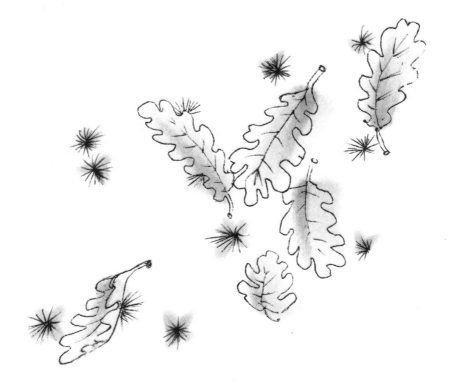

Finding Faith in a Flower

Sometimes when faith is running low
And I cannot fathom WHY THINGS ARE SO . . .
I walk alone among the flowers I grow
And learn the "ANSWERS" to ALL I WOULD
      KNOW!
For among my flowers I have come to see
Life's MIRACLE and its MYSTERY . . .
And standing in silence and reverie
My FAITH COMES FLOODING BACK TO ME!

Birthdays Are a Gift From God

Where does *time* go in its endless flight—
Spring turns to fall and day to night,
And birthdays come and birthdays go
And where they go we do not know . . .
But God who planned our life on earth
And gave our mind and body birth
And then enclosed a living soul
With heaven as the spirit's goal
Has given man the gift of choice
To follow that small inner voice
That speaks to us from year to year
Reminding us we've naught to fear . . .
For *birthdays* are a *stepping-stone*
To endless joys as yet unknown,
So fill each day with happy things
And may your burdens all take wings
And fly away and leave behind
Great joy of heart and peace of mind . . .
For *birthdays* are *the gateway* to
An *endless life of joy for you*
If you but pray from day to day
That He will show you the *Truth* and
      The Way.

Showers of Blessings

Each day
there are showers of blessings
sent from the Father Above,
For God is a great, lavish giver
and there is no end to His love—
His grace
is more than sufficient,
His mercy is boundless and deep,
And His infinite blessings
are countless
and all this we're given to keep,
If we but seek God
and find Him
and ask for a bounteous measure
Of this wholly immeasurable offering
from God's inexhaustible treasure—
For no matter
how big man's dreams are,
God's blessings are Infinitely more,
For always God's Giving
is greater
than what man is Asking for.

There's Sunshine in a Smile

Life is a mixture
      of sunshine and rain,
Laughter and pleasure,
      teardrops and pain,
All days can't be bright,
      but it's certainly true,
There was never a cloud
      the sun didn't shine through—
So just keep on smiling
      whatever betide you,
Secure in the knowledge
      God is always beside you,
And you'll find when you smile
      your day will be brighter
And all of your burdens
      will seem so much lighter—
For each time you smile
      you will find it is true
Somebody, somewhere
      will *smile back at you,*
And nothing on earth
      can make life more worthwhile
Than the sunshine and warmth
      of a *beautiful smile.*

Count Your Gains and Not Your Losses

As we travel down life's busy road
Complaining of our heavy load,
We often think God's been unfair
And gave us much more than our share
Of little daily irritations
And disappointing tribulations . . .
We're discontented with our lot
And all the "bad breaks" that we got,
We count our losses, not our gain,
And remember only tears and pain . . .
The good things we forget completely
When God looked down and blessed us sweetly,
Our troubles fill our every thought,
We dwell upon lost goals we sought,
And wrapped up in our own despair
We have no time to see or share
Another's load that far outweighs
Our little problems and dismays . . .
And so we walk with head held low
And little do we guess or know
That someone near us on life's street
Is burdened deeply with defeat . . .
But if we'd but forget *our care*
And stop in sympathy to share
The burden that "our brother" carried,
Our mind and heart would be less harried
And we would feel our load was small,
In fact, *we carried no load at all.*

Thank You, God, for Everything

Thank you, God, for everything—
      the big things and the small,
For "every good gift comes from God"—
      the giver of them all—
And all too often we accept
      without any thanks or praise
The gifts God sends as blessings
      each day in many ways,
And so at this *Thanksgiving time*
      we offer up a prayer
To thank you, God, for giving us
      a lot more than our share . . .
First, thank you for the little things
      that often come our way,
The things we take for granted
      but don't mention when we pray,
The unexpected courtesy,
      the thoughtful, kindly deed,
A hand reached out to help us
      in the time of sudden need . . .
Oh, make us more aware, dear God,
      of little daily graces
That come to us with "sweet surprise"
      from never-dreamed-of places—

Then, thank you for the *"Miracles"*
    we are much too blind to see,
And give us new awareness
    of our many gifts from Thee,
And help us to remember
    that the *Key* to *Life* and *Living*
Is to make each prayer a *Prayer of Thanks*
    and every day *Thanksgiving.*

A Prayer of Thanks

Thank You, GOD, for everything
      I've experienced here on earth—
Thank You for protecting me
      from the moment of my birth—
And thank You for the beauty
      around me everywhere,
The gentle rain and glistening dew,
      the sunshine and the air,
The joyous gift of "feeling"
      the soul's soft, whispering voice
That speaks to me from deep within
      and makes my heart rejoice—
Oh, GOD, no words are great enough
      to thank You for just living,
And that is why every day
      is a day for real THANKSGIVING.

Everyone Needs Someone

People need people and friends need friends,
And we all need love for a full life depends
Not on vast riches or great acclaim,
Not on success or on worldly fame,
But just in knowing that someone cares
And holds us close in their thoughts and prayers—
For only the knowledge that we're understood
Makes everyday living feel *wonderfully good,*
And we rob ourselves of life's greatest need
When we "lock up our hearts" and fail to heed
The outstretched hand reaching to find
A kindred spirit whose heart and mind
Are lonely and longing to somehow share
Our joys and sorrows and to make us aware
That life's completeness and richness depends
On the things we share with our loved ones and friends.

A Thankful Heart

Take nothing for granted,
     for whenever you do
The "joy of enjoying"
     is lessened for you—
For we rob our own lives
     much more than we know
When we fail to respond
     or in any way show
Our thanks for the blessings
     that daily are ours . . .
The warmth of the sun,
     the fragrance of flowers,
The beauty of twilight,
     the freshness of dawn,
The coolness of dew
     on a green velvet lawn,
The kind little deeds
     so thoughtfully done,
The favors of friends
     and the love that someone
Unselfishly gives us
     in a myriad of ways,

Expecting no payment
      and no words of praise—
Oh, great is our loss
      when we no longer find
A thankful response
      to things of this kind,
For the *joy of enjoying*
      and the *Fullness of living*
Are found in the heart
      that is filled with *Thanksgiving.*

Things to Be Thankful For

The good, green earth beneath our feet,
The air we breathe, the food we eat,
Some work to do, a goal to win,
A hidden longing deep within
That spurs us on to bigger things
And helps us meet what each day brings,
All these things and many more
Are things we should be thankful for . . .
And most of all our thankful prayers
Should rise to God because He cares!

"Climb 'til Your Dream Comes True"

Often your tasks will be many,
And more than you think you can do . . .
Often the road will be rugged
And the hills insurmountable, too . . .
But always remember,
the hills ahead
Are never as steep as they seem,
And with Faith in your heart
start upward
And climb 'til you reach your dream,
For nothing in life that is worthy
Is ever too hard to achieve
If you have the courage to try it
And you have the Faith to believe . . .
For Faith is a force that is greater
Than knowledge or power
or skill
And many defeats turn to triumph
If you trust in God's wisdom and will . . .
For Faith is a mover of mountains,
There's nothing that God cannot do,
So start out today
with Faith in your heart
And "Climb 'Til Your Dream Comes True"!

99

Ideals Are Like Stars

In this world of casual carelessness
it's discouraging to try
To keep our morals and standards
and our Ideals High . . .
We are ridiculed and laughed at
by the smart sophisticate
Who proclaims in brittle banter
that such things are
out of date . . .
But no life is worth the living
unless it's built on truth,
And we lay our life's foundation
in the golden years of youth . . .
So allow no one to stop you
or hinder you from laying
A firm and strong foundation
made of Faith and Love
and Praying . . .
And remember that Ideals
are like Stars Up In The Sky,
You can never really reach them,
hanging in the heavens high . . .

But like the mighty mariner
who sailed the storm-tossed sea,
And used the Stars To Chart
His Course
with skill and certainty,
You too can Chart Your Course in Life
With High Ideals and Love,
For High Ideals are like the Stars
that light the sky above . . .
You cannot ever
reach them,
but Lift Your Heart Up High
And your Life will be as Shining
as the Stars Up In The Sky.

Love Is a Heart Gift

LOVE is a HEART GIFT
      that cannot be BOUGHT OR SOLD
For any amount
      of SILVER or GOLD . . .
And there could never be another
      who LOVES MORE DEEPLY than a MOTHER!

A Favorite Recipe

Take a cup of *Kindness,* mix it well with *Love,*
Add a lot of *Patience* and *Faith* in *God above,*
Sprinkle very generously with *Joy* and *Thanks* and *Cheer*—
And you'll have lots of *"Angel Food"* to feast on all the
      year.

For One Who Gives
So Much to Others

It's not the things that can be bought
    that are life's richest treasure,
It's just the little "heart gifts"
    that money cannot measure . . .
A cheerful smile, a friendly word,
    a sympathetic nod
Are priceless little treasures
    from the storehouse of our God . . .
They are the things that can't be bought
    with silver or with gold,
For thoughtfulness and kindness
    and love are never sold . . .
They are the priceless things in life
    for which no one can pay,
And the giver finds rich recompense
    in *Giving Them Away*.
And who on earth gives more away
    and does more good for others
Than understanding, kind and wise
    and selfless, loving *Mothers*
Who ask no more than just the joy
    of helping those they love
To find in life the happiness
    that they are dreaming of.

"Flowers Leave Their Fragrance on the Hand That Bestows Them"

There's an old Chinese proverb
    that, if practiced each day,
Would change the whole world
    in a wonderful way—
Its truth is so simple,
    it's so easy to do,
And it works every time
    and successfully, too—
For you can't do a kindness
    without a reward,
Not in silver nor gold
    but in joy from the Lord—
You can't light a candle
    to show others the way
Without feeling the warmth
    of that bright little ray—
And you can't pluck a rose,
    all fragrant with dew,
Without part of its fragrance
    remaining with you . . .

And whose hands bestow
    more fragrant bouquets
Than Mother who daily
    speaks kind words of praise,
A Mother whose courage
    and comfort and cheer
Lights bright little candles
    in hearts through the year—
No wonder the hands
    of an Unselfish Mother
Are symbols of sweetness
    unlike any other.

No Other Love
Like Mother's Love

A Mother's love is something
     that no one can explain,
It is made of deep devotion
     and of sacrifice and pain,
It is endless and unselfish
     and enduring come what may
For nothing can destroy it
     or take that love away . . .
It is patient and forgiving
     when all others are forsaking,
And it never fails or falters
     even though the heart is breaking . . .
It believes beyond believing
     when the world around condemns,
And it glows with all the beauty
     of the rarest, brightest gems . . .
It is far beyond defining,
     it defies all explanation,
And it still remains a secret
     like the mysteries of creation . . .
A many splendored miracle
     man cannot understand
And another wondrous evidence
     of God's tender guiding hand.

Fathers Are Wonderful People

Fathers are wonderful people
  too little understood,
And we do not sing their praises
  as often as we should . . .
For, somehow, Father seems to be
  the man who pays the bills,
While Mother binds up little hurts
  and nurses all our ills . . .
And Father struggles daily
  to live up to *"his image"*
As protector and provider
  and "hero of the scrimmage" . . .
And perhaps that is the reason
  we sometimes get the notion
That Fathers are not subject
  to the thing we call emotion,
But if you look inside Dad's heart,
  where no one else can see,
You'll find he's sentimental
  and as "soft" as he can be . . .
But he's so busy every day
  in the grueling race of life,
He leaves the sentimental stuff
  to his partner and his wife . . .

But Fathers are just *wonderful*
        in a million different ways,
And they merit loving compliments
        and accolades of praise,
For the only reason Dad aspires
        to fortune and success
Is to make the family proud of him
        and to bring them happiness . . .
And like *Our Heavenly Father,*
        he's a guardian and a guide,
Someone that we can count on
        to be *always on our side.*

A Tribute to All Daughters

Every home should have a daughter,
    for there's nothing like a girl
To keep the world around her
    in one continuous whirl . . .
From the moment she arrives on earth,
    and on through womanhood,
A daughter is a *female*
    who is seldom understood . . .
One minute she is laughing,
    the next she starts to cry,
Man just can't understand her
    and there's just no use to try . . .
She is soft and sweet and cuddly,
    but she's also wise and smart,
She's a wondrous combination
    of a mind and brain and heart . . .
And even in her baby days
    she's just a born coquette,
And anything she really wants
    she manages to get . . .
For even at a tender age
    she uses all her wiles
And she can melt the hardest heart
    with the sunshine of her smiles . . .
She starts out as a rosebud
    with her beauty unrevealed,
Then through a happy childhood
    her petals are unsealed . . .

She's soon a sweet girl graduate,
    and then a blushing bride,
And then a lovely woman
    as the rosebud opens wide . . .
And some day in the future,
    if it be God's gracious will,
She, too, will be a Mother
    and know that reverent thrill
That comes to every Mother
    whose heart is filled with love
When she beholds the "angel"
    that God sent her from above . . .
And there would be no life at all
    in this world or the other
Without a *darling daughter*
    who, in turn, becomes a *Mother!*

A Prayer for the Young and Lovely

Dear God, I keep praying
For the things I desire,
You tell me I'm selfish
And "playing with fire"—
It is hard to believe
I am selfish and vain,
My desires seem so real
And my needs seem so sane,
And yet You are wiser
And Your vision is wide
And You look down on me
And You see deep inside,
You know it's so easy
To change and distort,
And things that are evil
Seem so harmless a sport—
Oh, teach me, dear God,
To not rush ahead
But to pray for Your guidance
And to trust You instead,

For You know what I need
And that I'm only a slave
To the things that I want
And desire and crave—
Oh, God, in your mercy
Look down on me now
And see in my heart
That I love you somehow,
Although in my rashness,
Impatience and greed
I pray for the things
That I *want* and *don't need*—
And instead of a *crown*
Please send me a *cross*
And teach me to know
That *all Gain* is but *loss*,
And show me the way
To joy without end,
With You as my *Father,*
Redeemer and *Friend*—
And send me the things
That are hardest to bear,
And keep me forever
Safe in Thy care.

God Bless America

"America the beautiful"—
May it always stay that way—
But to keep *"Old Glory"* flying
There's a price that we must pay . . .
For everything worth having
Demands work and sacrifice,
And *freedom* is a *Gift* from *God*
That commands the *highest price* . . .
For all our wealth and progress
Are as worthless as can be
Without the *Faith* that made us great
And kept *our country free* . . .
Nor can our nation hope to live
Unto itself alone,
For the problems of our neighbors
Must today become our own . . .
And while it's hard to understand
The complexities of war,
Each one of us must realize
That we are fighting for
The principles of freedom
And the decency of man,
And as a Christian Nation
We're committed to God's Plan . . .

And as the *Land* of *Liberty*
And a great God-fearing nation
We must protect our honor
And fulfill our obligation . . .
So in these times of crisis
Let us offer no resistance
In giving help to those who need
Our strength and our assistance—
And *"The Stars and Stripes Forever"*
Will remain a symbol of
A rich and mighty nation
Built on *Faith* and *Truth* and *Love*.

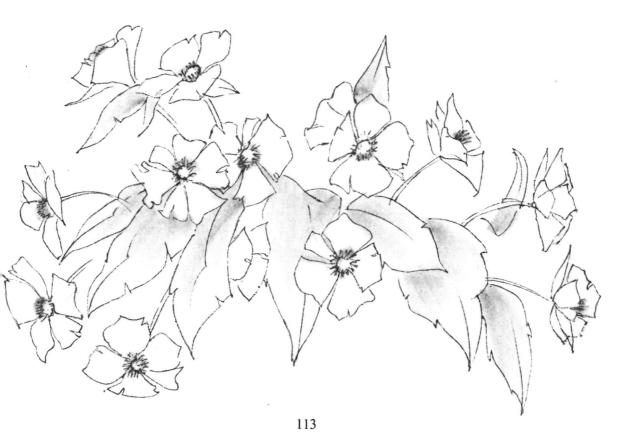

A Tribute to J.F.K.

His gallant soul has but taken flight
      into 'the land where there is no night'
He is not dead,
      he has only gone on
Into a brighter
      and more wonderful dawn . . .
For his passion for justice
      among men of good will
No violence can silence,
      no bullet can still . . .
For his spirit lives on
      and, like the warm sun,
It will nourish the dreams
      that he had begun . . .

So this hour of sorrow
      is only God's will,
For the 'good in this man
      is living here still' . . .
Forgive our transgressions
      and revive us anew
So we may draw closer
      to each other and YOU . . .
For unless 'God is guard,'
      John Kennedy said,
'We're standing unguarded'
      with dreams that are dead . . .

For a nation too proud
      to kneel down and pray
Will crumble to chaos
      and descend to decay . . .
So use 'WHAT HE GAVE'
      for a REDEDICATION
And make this once more
      a God-fearing nation—
A symbol of hope—and
      a standard for good
As we lead in the struggle
      for a 'NEW BROTHERHOOD'!

Out of My Life

Little Lights and Shadows from My Present and Past
as told to
DONALD T. KAUFFMAN

Not long ago I received a letter from a man who asked me what I had done to "meet life successfully." As I tried to explain to him, I am a very ordinary person. I do not think of myself as a success, but as just another worker in God's vineyard. The phenomenal sale of my books and writings is not due to anything special about me or my way of living. It is a tribute to the wonderful goodness of God, not to me; at best, I am just an instrument for His message. This short account of my life has been written, at the publishers' request, not to publicize any "success secrets," but to show how completely God helps us solve our problems when we place ourselves completely in His mighty hands.

I was born in the bustling little town of Lorain, Ohio, on the shore of Lake Erie. Lorain is a busy lakeport; its steel mill is still one of the largest in the United States. Everyone in town was pretty much on an equal level socially, and my sister Gertrude and I had a very happy childhood.

My father, John A. Steiner, was a railroad engineer and a marvelous man. I never heard him swear once or lose his temper. My mother was high-spirited, but my father was always gentle and calm; he was just a very nice person. There was not an ounce of bias in him—he was as much at home with a Lake Erie fisherman as he would have been with the President. He loved to hunt, and he invited everyone from bankers to street cleaners to come hunting with him.

Mother had an exceptional flair for making lovely clothes. Everyone said that I had the most beautiful clothes in the world, and for this all the credit goes to my dear mother. She was ambitious for her children; she wanted us to be well educated and to have the better things of life. But Papa and I felt we already had everything important, and we were content with life.

When I was sixteen and a senior in high school, the bottom dropped out of my life. Papa died in a flu epidemic. Although we were not destitute, I felt that I ought to do something to help my mother and younger sister, and I started thinking about a job.

I did not have to think about it long. I was offered work by the Lorain branch of the Ohio Public Service Company, first as a "pinch hitter" and then in other jobs for which I volunteered. Before long I was director of public relations for Public Service and chairman of the women's committee on public relations for the National Electric Light Association (East Central Division).

One day I was asked to speak at an electric light convention at Cedar Point. When I got to the platform I thought to myself, *I don't really know how to start this, or what to say, or even how much.* I panicked a bit—then another thought came into my mind:

Your Father knows.

Then and there, in that split fraction of a second, I spoke to the God who means everything to me. I said, "I don't know what to do, Father—You tell me."

At that moment a wonderful feeling of assurance and confidence swept over me; I knew that my heavenly Father was answering.

There were a lot of businessmen at the convention. I picked out one who looked friendly and understanding and started talking to him and, from the response I could see in his face, I knew that what I wanted to say was getting across. Other faces started to respond, and when I finished, there was a long round of applause.

I have always spoken in public just as I would talk to someone in my living room. I never tried to make a name for myself, or to use big words, so I never had the tension and struggle of getting too involved with myself. I learned to let go and to let God take control.

There were many things I was anxious to speak about. Women's rights were a constant topic while I was growing up; all my teachers had been suffragettes, and I firmly believed in the right and ability of women to win their own way in the world. I developed a number of lecture topics like "Blue Eyes or Gray Matter" and "Living and Working Enthusiastically."

I discovered that many men were ready and willing to listen to an enthusiastic presentation of these matters by a blonde young lady who knew how to appeal to their sense of humor as well as to their business interests and their sense of fair play.

I began receiving more and more invitations to speak. I addressed the American Electric Railway Convention (a very big thing at that time) in Washington, D.C. There I was photographed with President Calvin Coolidge. B. C. Forbes, publisher of *Forbes Magazine,* wrote me, "The place for you is not Lorain, Ohio, but some metropolitan city like New York where there is so much more room for doing big things." I had a number of statements of this kind printed in a circular, prepared a list of lecture topics, and started my own lecture circuit.

As long as I live, I'll remember the speech I made at the Statler Hotel in Buffalo, New York. (Mr. Storr, head of the Buffalo Board of Education, had read an interview with me in *Nation's Business* and had invited me to address a business luncheon at the Statler.)

When I arrived at the room where the luncheon was being held, everything was buzzing. I had never seen so many people in a room that size. I didn't know what Mr. Storr looked like, nor where I was to go; I guess I felt a little lost.

I approached a man at what looked like the head table and said, "I would like to talk to Mr. Storr."

The man replied, "You can't see him now. He's busy—he's hunting for the speaker."

I said, "I am the speaker."

The man was visibly upset. I thought he was going to collapse! He went away and returned soon with a large, imposing-looking gentleman who looked at me in such a way that, if I could have shriveled up under his gaze, I surely would have.

Finally he said, "There has been a mistake. We asked the woman who was photographed with President Coolidge to speak here. You are just a child!"

I *was* quite small and slender, and I was wearing a little gold two-piece dress with a purple toque pulled down over my forehead. At that time, dresses were *very* short, and Mr. Storr looked as if he thought I was a schoolgirl who had lost her way.

I said, "I'm it."

Mr. Storr tried awfully hard to be nice to me, but it was obviously a hardship. He said, "I don't think you can make yourself heard here. Have you ever talked to this many people?"

"Oh, yes," I said. "This room is really small compared to the Chamber of Commerce Hall where I spoke in Washington."

Mr. Storr said, "We've invited the whole John Larkin Company to this luncheon. John Larkin is here himself! I do hope you won't disappoint us."

What a way to build up confidence! But I asked my Father for help—as I have learned to do every time I make a speech or write a poem—and, at the end of my speech, Mr. Storr said, "I never would have believed you could do it." I must say that he did everything in his power to make up for the way he had greeted me. He escorted me to all the local attractions and sent me an enormous box of roses.

One evening I spoke to the Annual Clearinghouse Association of Bankers at the Dayton Country Club on the topic, "Do You Know Your Job or Do You *Love* Your Job?" The member delegated to meet the speaker was a tall, handsome young man named Franklin D. Rice. After the meeting, he asked me, "Would you like to go someplace and have something to eat?" Many of those present kidded me about going out with the most eligible bachelor in Dayton, Ohio.

Franklin, I learned, had been a Lieutenant in the Air Force in World War I. And when I first met him, he was an officer with the Dayton Savings and Trust Company. He commuted a great deal to New York, and came of a family of outstanding ability and wealth. In a year we were married.

Everyone said that I was the luckiest girl in the world, and I had to agree. For our honeymoon Franklin had arranged a cruise through the Caribbean. We had a beautiful suite on an enormous luxury liner.

About a week after the cruise began, Franklin began getting daily cablegrams from his banking associates. The stock market was beginning to fall and the Great Depression was beginning. But Franklin never allowed himself to be anything but the perfect husband and host, gay and friendly to all aboard. Instead of panicking over Wall Street's crash, he followed the usually sound practice of buying while others were selling. He kept wiring his bank to buy more and more stock.

For the next two years we lived more extravagantly than ever. Suspecting the truth, I wanted to let our servants go and return to work, but Franklin would not hear of it. "Do you want to advertise to the whole world that things are slipping?" he asked. "We must put up a good front no matter what happens."

Finally everything Franklin D. Rice had owned was gone. Then, one terrible gray morning, I woke up to find that Franklin was gone too. About all he left me was a note in which he had written:

> Darling, The only thing I'm sorry about is that I never could give you all the things I meant to. I hope you believe that I really wanted to give them to you, and I could have given them to you before everything went. . . .

You'll always go on. I only knew one world. I just can't go down and become a bum—I have to go out with the bands playing.

After my husband's tragic death, the officers of the Gibson Company asked me to work for them. When I asked what they wanted me to do, they said, "Just come and you'll find out."

The first thing they asked me to do was to make a general survey of the offices and tell them what to do to improve their greeting card business. Of course I had recommendations galore! I stylized the cards and formed various programs. Then the editor suddenly contracted pneumonia and died, and E. P. Gibson (the company's founder), his nephew J. R. Gibson, and the other officers asked me to become the new editor. Although I protested that I had never written a rhyme in my life, they said, "Just take the job until we get someone."

There is nothing about my life that I have really planned. I am a very definite believer in the philosophy of Christ: "Consider the lilies, how they grow." I think you have to be willing to work hard and do whatever job is put before you. I don't think you can just sit down and say, "I don't want that because I want to be the head of it all." I have never been the head of anything. I always start out trying to do the job I have been given—and I always see a lot more in the job than what it had when I began it.

Still, *God's* plan is wonderful. And His timing is perfect. I always leaned toward a clear expression of faith in the cards I produced; I don't believe in keeping inside what you believe about God. He is no one to be ashamed of! But it never became possible for my poems to be published until a few years ago. I am convinced that if they had been published when I wanted them to be, they would not have found ready acceptance. *Now* is the time the world so desperately needs these messages of faith and inspiration, and people would not have responded to them previously, as they do today. The world is in such turmoil now that a great many men and women and young people are ready to listen to the message.

Millions of my poems have now been printed, and the first compilation of them ever published has sold more than 700,000 copies in less than seven years. And its seventh printing sells just as well as the newest volume off the press.

As many of my readers know, Lawrence Welk selected my poem "The Priceless Gift of Christmas" for reading on his television show, and this produced thousands of new customers for my work. That reading by Aladdin was a marvelous answer to prayer, as I pointed out in my poem "How It All Happened."

Six years ago on *The Lawrence Welk Show*
An artist whom so many folks know
Received a card with a Christmas verse
That spoke of *The Holy Christ Child's Birth*—
And for some reason it caught his eye,
And I doubt today that he even knows *Why*.
For the reader and writer had never met
But the writer is one who will never forget
The joyous amazement and rapt surprise
When out of the starlit Christmas skies
Across the country from shore to shore
An unknown verse never heard before
Was heard by millions of listening ears,
And the writer's dream of many years
Was answered by God in a wonderful way,
And from that night to this present day
Aladdin still reads with his magic touch
The verses that people have liked so much—
And while it may look like a happenstance,
Or something born of a lucky chance,
The writer is sure that God drew the plan
And put it into the hands of man.
And, Aladdin,
    one of *the Lawrence Welk band*,
Just carried out what the Lord had planned—
For I had prayed for many long years
Through disappointments and often tears
To find, without attempts to preach,
A way that I could somehow reach
Responsive hearts . . . much like *my own*
And tell them *"No One Walks Alone"*—
But little did I guess or know
My prayer would be answered on
    The Lawrence Welk Show,
For since *"The Priceless Gift"* was aired,
Through *Aladdin's voice* I've often shared
All the verses between these covers.
And through the years there may be others
That I can share with folks like you

For there's *nothing* I would rather do—
And this is *the story* of *"How it Began"*
Six years ago with "The Music Man."

A year later my poem "The Praying Hands" was read on the Welk show. Then, early in 1962, John Glenn became the first American to orbit the earth, and his remarkable testimony of faith in God inspired and delighted millions who had been thrilled by his historic flight. I composed a poem of tribute to John's mother, which was read by Aladdin that Mother's Day. John Glenn's mother wrote me:

> I received your lovely poem . . . I am so thrilled by it, I hardly know how to write to you. It is beautiful. . . . I plan to have the copy you sent me framed, and keep it always.

From all over the world I received wonderful letters about my poems. A delegate to the United Nations took one of my books back to Bombay, and his secretary read it. She wrote me a glowing letter of appreciation, adding:

> At present there is a problem about our home which I (and my parents) are most worried about and we all are most earnestly praying about it. At first, I guess, worry was a block, which made me, too, have a feeling that my prayers were not getting through. Now, even though the outcome is not evident, I am knowing, as you so well put it, "No matter in what guise or disguise things come to us, they are sent for our good from Our Father."
>
> I just thought I would let you know how very much your letters and poems help me.

A woman in Minnesota wrote:

> You are causing people to pause, weigh values, and turn to the God who made us, when we need to be sustained—when our "original batteries" need recharging!

A secretary wrote of my book *Just for You:*

> By the time I finished reading it, I felt as if I could move mountains, or withstand one falling on me. I wish everyone had the opportunity to read this certainly unforgettable book.

A Kentucky lady wrote:

In the past year I have read any and all of your poems I could get ahold of. Without you and your beautiful poetry to remind me constantly of God's love, I don't know where I would be—perhaps even dead—yes, even killed by my own hand. Your beautiful poetry has reminded me every hour of every day how much God cares.

You see, I have leukemia, and have a year—perhaps two—to live. And all of a sudden I was terribly frightened. I shouldn't be, I know—God was close—He had always been—and yet I felt that all of a sudden He had forgotten me.

Then—Helen Steiner Rice—I read "The End of The Road Is But a Bend in The Road," and all of a sudden I felt better. I read every poem of yours that I could get ahold of, and with each one I felt better until I'm not afraid anymore—I am closer to God than ever before, and when my time comes—I'm ready.

Another person wrote me about a cousin who was in prison:

This man had done a wrong and is paying for it at this time at the Indiana State Prison. He happens to be a cousin of mine. Since I believe in the human race I write to this man and try to encourage him. And believe you me he needs all the encouragement he can get. You may be interested to know that one way I have for doing this is to buy the most beautiful verses by Helen Steiner Rice that I can find. Not only does he get a lot of good and encouragement from these but I read and reread them myself before I send them and they give me the special lift that we all need every now and then.

I spend a lot of time replying to letters like these. Probably seventy-five percent of them are from people in small towns or villages, or from lonely dwellers on prairies or in apartments. A dear little grandmother wrote me that after buying my book *Just For You* she bought seven copies for her children, and then four copies for other relatives, and then six more to give to friends! She said:

I will never get tired of reading your poems. They have brought me closer to God and have renewed my faith and given me new hope and love. I only pray every night that God will bless you with lots of good health so you can

124

keep on writing forever and doing His work.

God does bless me with *countless* blessings. But I don't want anyone to think that I'm always happy and on top of the world. Sometimes I feel like an empty, dried-out corn husk. But, as Jimmie Davis sings, "You've got to keep on walking." Many days I say to my marvelously efficient secretary, "Mary Jo, today I feel as flat and drained out as though a ten-ton truck just ran over me. But we've got to keep going, because if we don't, we're not going to keep up with the schedule!"

Each morning before I go to my office I say this little prayer:

> Bless me, heavenly Father,
>   forgive my erring ways,
> Grant me strength to serve Thee,
>   put purpose in my days . . .
> Give me understanding
>   enough to make me kind
> So I may judge all people
>   with my heart and not my mind . . .
> And teach me to be patient
>   in everything I do,
> Content to trust your wisdom
>   and to follow after You . . .
> And help me when I falter
>   and hear me when I pray
> And receive me in *Thy Kingdom*
>   to dwell with Thee some day.

Many times, during the day, I find occasion to repeat two of the lines: "Teach me to be *patient*" and *"Help me when I falter!"*

As I think back over the wonderful years I have enjoyed, I truly feel that many people are not really living—that somehow they miss the beauty and joy and goodness that God has put all around them. If my poems do anything, I believe they help people find the satisfaction of living life to its fullest. God's gifts are all around us, but so many people who receive them don't seem to be aware of them, and sometimes it seems to me that they never fully enjoy them.

Living is like breathing. I want to breathe deep so I can live! And it's possible to miss the joy of filling our lungs with fresh clean air, as well as the joy of living each moment to its fullest.

My own life has overflowed with happiness. And God has taught me the blessed secret of finding His purposes in even tragically black moments. Even the events that are unhappiest pass away and turn into things that are really wonderful. I can't waste my time thinking about things that are sad, because there are so many good things in life. Why should I dwell on the things that would only make me unhappy?

Whenever anyone thanks me for one of my books or poems, I have to give all the credit to God. I don't have much to do with these poems, really. Everything I write is borrowed—it's from God, and from His age-old wisdom. I'm only an instrument for getting His message into people's lives. God gives me the ability to put it down, then He directs the traffic and gets my verse into the hands and hearts of people who find their own souls reflected in what I write.

As I said on one interview show, I have the best material in the world to work with, so nothing can compete with it! How can anyone do better than repeat the simple old words of faith and hope and kindness and love? Everything in the world may change, but these things are always valid.

Sometimes cynical people ask me what proof I have of these invisible realities I write about. What more proof could there be than what God puts all around us? Spiritual reality is like the air. You can't see it, but you can feel it; you know it is there and you couldn't live without it. I like to get up early in the morning and enjoy the wonderful songs of the birds and the smell of the flowers and trees. Then, when I walk into my office, I ask,

> Who but God could make the day
> And gently tuck the night away?

At times, I must confess, I have wondered why I had to lose my husband, Franklin, so tragically, after just the two short years we had together. Only in the last three or four years have I been sure why it was permitted to happen as it did.

The night before Franklin and I were married, I told the story of a young girl who stood at the edge of a field of waving corn—a beautiful field, where every stalk was tall and green and luxuriant and every ear was perfect. And the farther the girl could see into the field, the larger the ears became.

A genie told the girl, "If you walk through this field, I will reward you with a gift in proportion to the size of the ear you select. There is only one restriction. You must start right where you are standing, and you may go through the field only once. You may not retrace your steps. The ear of corn you bring out will determine the reward you will receive on the other side of the field."

The girl was supremely happy as she started into the field. Carelessly she trod on many of the stalks, thinking to herself: *I won't take any of these, for in the center of the field are the most perfect ears of all. I want the biggest reward I can get.*

The girl ran on and on, intent on finding the largest ear in the field. Suddenly she realized that the corn stalks were getting smaller and thinner; she was nearing the far edge of the field. In desperation, she looked for a good ear, but she could not bring herself to pick any of those in sight. She kept thinking, *There's got to be another big ear before the end.* But there was not. She came out of the field empty-handed.

I realize now, more surely than ever before, that *things* can never bring happiness. So many people always look for something bigger and better, and as soon as they get one thing, they set their hearts on another. Happiness is, for them, a mink coat or a Cadillac—something big, something splashy. If someone shakes hands with them and says "God bless you," sincerely, they fail to realize that they have just received one of the greatest gifts there is.

If you take the love and friendship and the "God bless you's" that come your way, you have everything. The person who gets the mink coat receives nothing really worthwhile or lasting. But the true gifts of God can never be lost.

Surely, only love can heal this sick, tired world. But God stands ready through His Son to turn this Cross into a Crown—if we will but let Him warm our cold hearts with His love.

I firmly believe that,

> Great is the power
> of might and mind,
> *But Only Love*
> *Can Make Us Kind . . .*
> And all we are
> or hope to be
> is empty pride
> and vanity . . .
> if love is not
> a part of all,
> *The Greatest Man*
> *Is Very Small!*

Yes,

> Love is the language every heart speaks
> And Love is the answer to all that man seeks.

"Heart Gifts"

It's not the things that can be bought
    that are life's richest treasure,
It's just the little "heart gifts"
    that money cannot measure . . .
A cheerful smile, a friendly word,
    a sympathetic nod
Are priceless little treasures
    from the storehouse of our God . . .
They are the things that can't be bought
    with silver or with gold,
For thoughtfulness and kindness
    and love are never sold . . .
They are the priceless things in life
    for which no one can pay,
And the giver finds rich recompense
    in *giving them away.*

"Out of My Life" as told to Donald T. Kaufmann is excerpted from *Heart Gifts From Helen Steiner Rice.* Copyright © 1968 by Fleming H. Revell Company.